Occasional Paper of the
Camden History Society

Agar Town:
The Life & Death of a Victorian "Slum"

Steven L J Denford

Abstract

AGAR TOWN – a small estate developed from 1840 in the area to the east and north of St Pancras Old Church – was a squalid slum, housing many poor Irish who had been squeezed out of more central districts such as St Giles. Or so the history books tell us. But modern historians have simply recycled Victorian accounts. An influential article in Dickens' *Household Words*, March 1851, called Agar Town a suburban Irish slum. Others compared it to a gold-rush shanty town or a decayed rural village. This is not, however, the picture which emerges from a study of records such as deeds, the Vestry minutes, the census and poor law records.

This book describes the actual development of the area, considering the site and its surroundings – which were not such that a slum was inevitable – and the role of the Agar family, including the once infamous "Councillor" William Agar and his battle in earlier years with the Regent's Canal Company. His widow's decision to let off the land in small plots on 21-year leases did preclude a good class of development. Most plots were taken by working men escaping the appalling housing conditions nearer central London. The agreements for leases had numerous conditions attached, and the builders involved were working men who often continued to live in the houses they had built, which could otherwise command high rents. In the London of the day housing conditions in Agar Town were at worst unremarkable.

As to the inhabitants of Agar Town, contemporary writers saw them as typical slumland types – poor, drunken and Irish. Census, poor law and other records do not back this up. Only a tiny number claimed outdoor relief or sought admission to the nearby Workhouse, and disease was not rife. Very few of its inhabitants had been born in Ireland.

Falsely portrayed as a foul slum housing a depraved population, Agar Town fell easy prey to the Midland Railway Company, who without difficulty obtained Parliamentary powers and in 1866 swiftly demolished the area in order to build their line into the new St Pancras station, leaving the inhabitants to find other accommodation wherever they could.

I believe that Victorian social topographers unfairly 'labelled' Agar Town as part of a campaign to reform housing conditions generally.

The book concludes with a brief description of the subsequent fate of the area, now home to Camley Street Natural Park and, to the north, Elm Village.

© Steven L J Denford 1995

ISBN 0-904491-35-8

Contents

Published by the
Camden History Society

c/o Camden Libraries,
Holborn Branch,
32 Theobalds Road,
London WC1X 8PA

Editor: F Peter Woodford
Designer: Ivor Kamlish

Printed by:
Printpoint Ltd
Broadfield Lane
York Way
London NW1 9YS

	Key to abbreviations	4
1:	Introduction	5
2:	Before Agar Town	6
3:	Working class housing in early Victorian London	9
4:	The image of Agar Town	10
5:	Agar Town – a slum?	12
6:	The development of Agar Town	14
7:	The people of Agar Town	20
8:	The railway and Agar Town	23
9:	Agar Town – an assessment	26
10:	Agar Town today	27
Annex 1:	Article in *Household Words*, 1851	29
Annex 2:	Case study of ground rents in a part of Agar Town	31
	Bibliography	32

Key to abbreviations

B/NTG	Deeds reference in Greater London Record Office	GNR	Great Northern Railway	MRC	Midland Railway Company
CHL	Camden History (Local Studies) Library	HC	Heal Collection in CHL – references numbered in a series entitled BI	PP	Parliamentary Papers
GLRO	Greater London Record Office	Middx Reg	Middlesex Deeds Register at GLRO	VM	St Pancras Vestry minutes

1: Introduction

SEARCHING for Agar Town now is not easy. Virtually nothing remains above ground to bear witness to its short-lived existence in the quarter-century from 1840. The name is not on the map; the street now named Agar Grove, to the north of what was Agar Town, recalls the family which owned the land on which it developed. Yet in the mid-19th century Agar Town was notorious, a by-word for squalor, a shanty town that had sprung up overnight and had quickly become a foul and squalid slum, home to a depraved, mainly Irish population. This was the image popularised by housing reformers and contemporary social topographers, such as Beames in *The Rookeries of London* (1852)* and Hollingshead in *Ragged London* (1861). The image was so powerful that when in 1866 the Midland railway swept away Agar Town in just two months there was no public outcry, quite the reverse. Its destruction was a classic example of the power of the railway companies in Victorian London to wipe out working-class housing.

This book provides a history of the rise and fall of Agar Town and tries to counter some of the more sensational contemporary descriptions of the area. It is impossible to re-create the exact conditions under which people lived, but I hope to show that the housing process in Agar Town was much more complex than earlier commentators have suggested and its population was not the 'lowest of the low'. Agar Town, for all its faults, was – by the standards of the time – a realistic response by working men to a chronic housing shortage.

The genesis of this book was a thesis completed in 1994 for a master's degree in London Studies at Birkbeck College, University of London. The thesis, *Agar Town: Working Class Response to Housing Need*, describes the process in more detail and the interested reader is referred to the Camden Local Studies Library in the Holborn Public Library, 32 Theobalds Road, London WC1X 8PA, where a copy is deposited. I was drawn to study this area by the cursory yet intriguing references by modern historians to Agar Town in accounts of Victorian slums. To find out more I turned to local histories of St Pancras but found to my surprise that no detailed study of the area had been undertaken. There is only one short book devoted to Agar Town, a 1935 work by Rev. R Conyers Morrell, who had an antiquarian's interest in the area before it was built over, and is primarily concerned with ecclesiastical history. Much of the book deals with the church of St Thomas in what Morrell calls 'New Agar Town', ie the Wrotham Road area of Camden Town, where the Midland Railway Company paid for a new church after the destruction of Agar Town proper. There is no real analysis of the development of Agar Town in the 1840s. In fact he incorrectly states that the first leases were let in 1831.

More rewarding is the *Heal Collection*, a rich mine of maps, documents, illustrations and newscuttings on St Pancras bequeathed to the public library by Ambrose Heal (1847-1913). One can glean a good deal about contemporary opinion about Agar Town from this. Another source is local newspapers such as *The Metropolitan* and *The Camden and Kentish Towns Gazette*, and national papers such as *The Times* and housing journals such as *The Builder*.

The development of Agar Town can be charted by study of the minutes of the St Pancras Vestry. The Vestry was the local government authority of the day. It met regularly in the 1840s and even more frequently after the re-organisation of local government in 1855. The twice-yearly lists of new houses taken into rate assessment give a detailed picture of the growth of the built-up area, and rate appeals and assessments give a good idea of the standing of the properties in Agar Town. Maps and deeds are also essential to understand the way housing developed.

To get an idea of the type of people who lived in the area I have studied other records, including census records and poor law and health reports. Parliamentary records for the period after 1850 when concern for the condition of Agar Town first arose, such as the Report of the Board of Health in 1851 on the sanitary condition of Agar Town, are also a useful source to help piece together a picture of this now forgotten area.

* For complete bibliography see p. 32.

2: Before Agar Town

AGAR TOWN was developed on the prebendal manor of St Pancras, attached to St Paul's Cathedral. As defined in the Heal Collection document AI 122, a prebend is "an endowment in land, or pension in money, given to a cathedral or conventual church for the maintenance for a secular priest or regular canon, who was a prebendary as supported by the said prebend". Miller (1874) states that the manor of St Pancras included both Somers Town and Agar Town, but this conflates the lay manor with the prebendal manor. The prebendal manor, as distinct from the lay manor, lay between King's Road (now St Pancras Way) on the west (alongside the River Fleet, piped underground from 1825) and Maiden Lane (now York Way) on the east, extending north to the line of St Paul's Road (now Agar Grove) and south to what became the grounds of the Imperial Gas Light and Coke Company – just south of present Goods Way. However, the eastern portion, known in the 16th century as Allensbury, was owned by St Bartholomew's Hospital, and by the 18th century was no longer part of the manor. It eventually became the site of the Great Northern Railway (GNR) goods yard. Figure 1 shows the area today.

Agar Town was to develop on the western part of the prebendal manor. There was very little building on these lands before 1800. John Rocque's map (Fig.2) shows the area in 1745. 'Pancras' is a hamlet in the fields to the NNW of Battle Bridge (which became King's Cross in 1835) and The Bruel (roughly the site of St Pancras station now). The River Fleet can be clearly seen. The only buildings shown are St Pancras Old Church with its churchyard, the Adam and Eve tea garden a little to the north of it, and Pancras Wells and its pleasure grounds immediately to the south. St Pancras Workhouse, not moved to its present site until 1809, lies further along the road leading to Kentish Town (King's Road). One of the cluster of buildings here, to the east of the road, would have been the ruins of the old manor house of Pancras, once known as Chanler (HC BI 41), and said to have been the residence of Judge Jeffries.

The manor was leased by successive prebendaries of St Pancras, with renewal usually every 7 years. From 1755 the lease of the manor was in the Newcome (or Newcombe) family. In 1810 they decided to sell it at Garraway's Auction House and the purchaser of the estate of some 70 acres was Mr William Agar.

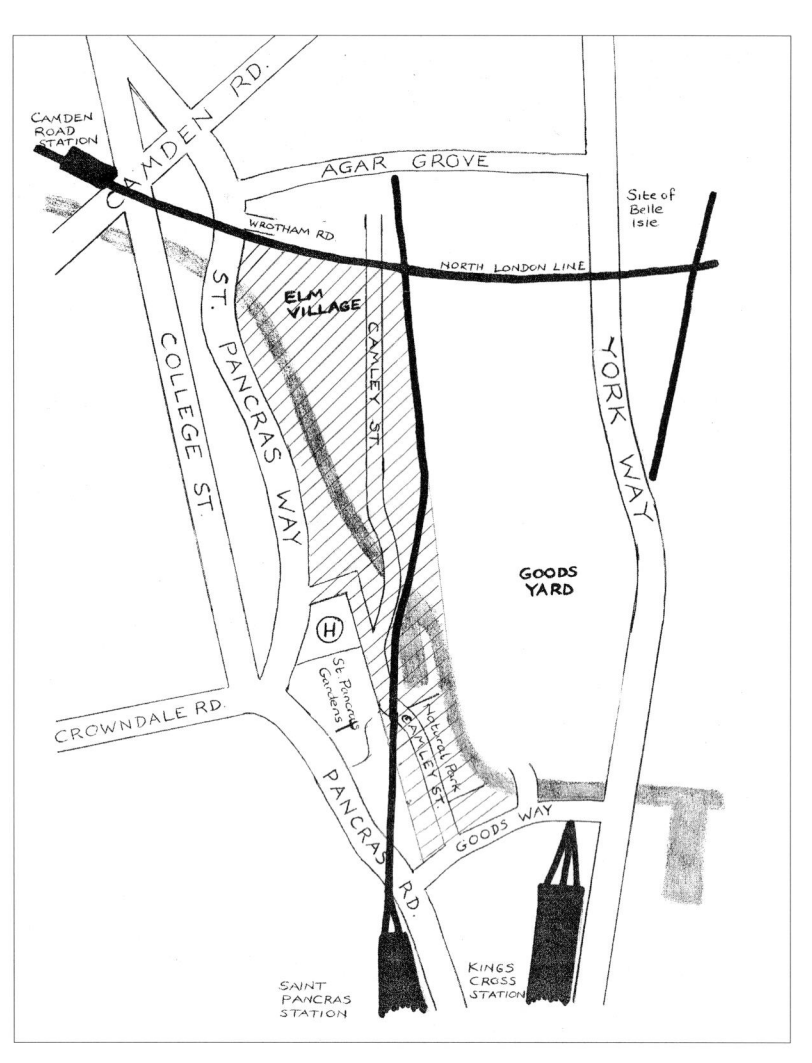

William Agar and The Regent's Canal

William Agar (1767-1838) was a lawyer in the Court of Chancery. Called to the Bar in 1791, he was later made a King's Counsellor and is often referred to as Counsellor Agar, sometimes incorrectly and confusingly written as Councillor. Agar (Fig.3) has had a very bad press. Some historians blame him for creating Agar Town, although he was dead by the time the first leases were let in 1840. He is perhaps better known for his attempts to thwart the Regent's Canal Company from running the canal through his newly acquired land.

There is a possibility that he was playing a double game here. The line of the canal was first mooted in 1802 by Thomas Homer, who in 1811 secured the help of (among others) the architect John Nash to realise the scheme. The Hon George Charles Agar is listed as one of the Proprietors of the Regent's Canal in the 1812 Regent's Canal Act. This Mr Agar would no doubt have known of Homer's plans some years before. He may have been a relative of William Agar, who purchased the lease of the land in 1810 perhaps intending to profit from its potential value as industrial sites. William Agar certainly sold his interest in the southern portion of the estate in 1822 to the Imperial Gas, Light & Coke Company, which used the canal to transport the great quantities of coal it required.

And yet at the same time Agar fought a battle – which literally came to blows – against the Regent's Canal Company to prevent his land being used for the canal.

Agar kept up his campaign against the Company for many years. He had petitioned against the Bill in 1812, and in 1813 had protested to the Company against the surveyors' entry onto his lands to stake out the line of the canal. In January 1814 Agar obtained an injunction to restrain them from injuring his house and grounds. The 1812 Act said it was not lawful for the Commissioners to injure any house or ground laid out before 1 January 1811 without the consent of the proprietor, except in cases mentioned in the Schedule to the Act – and Agar's lands had not been mentioned. In March 1814 Agar was awarded £2,600 in compensation by the Grand Jury, but he was in court again in November and December saying that the company were deviating from the line described in the Act. The Lord Chancellor asked Agar to set out what he thought was the right line, but shortly afterwards Agar was seeking, unsuccessfully, to commit company officials to the Fleet Prison for a supposed disobedience to the court in setting out this line.

In 1815 the company surveyor, Morgan, gave notice that he intended to survey the land and ignored Agar's letter of protest. Agar ordered his gardeners and servants to barricade the gateway. Morgan's men used barrows and planks to force an entry, then started digging. Bow Street officers were called the next day. Local magistrates dismissed Agar's complaint but he issued a writ in the Court of Exchequer against the Chairman of the company and several of the employees. The latter were found guilty and Agar was awarded further compensation of £1500.

Lord Stanhope then undertook his own negotiations with Agar to avoid further litigation. But in July 1816 Agar claimed that he had not received the damages to which he was entitled and was back in court again in 1817 taking action against the company for deviating from the agreed line.

Fig. 1 (p.6) Sketch map of the area today

Fig. 2 (left) Rocque's map of 1745

Fig. 3 (below) William Agar KC. Artist and date not recorded (Camden Local Studies Library)

Fig. 4 (bottom) Agar's House, Elm Lodge, drawn by a Mr King in the Kentish Town Roll (1840s, referring to period around 1820). Other pictures, eg Fig. 5, show a Georgian building with a bowfronted bay on the entrance front; the turreted effect here results from an unfortunate attempt by the artist to portray the treetops behind the house. (Camden Local Studies Library)

Agar's aim at all times appears to have been to get more money for himself. On one occasion he even tried to take a James Cochrane to court for damaging his crops, when Cochrane was assessing the value of the crops so the company could offer compensation! In 1818 Agar received compensation totalling £15,750.

Agar got personal recompense from

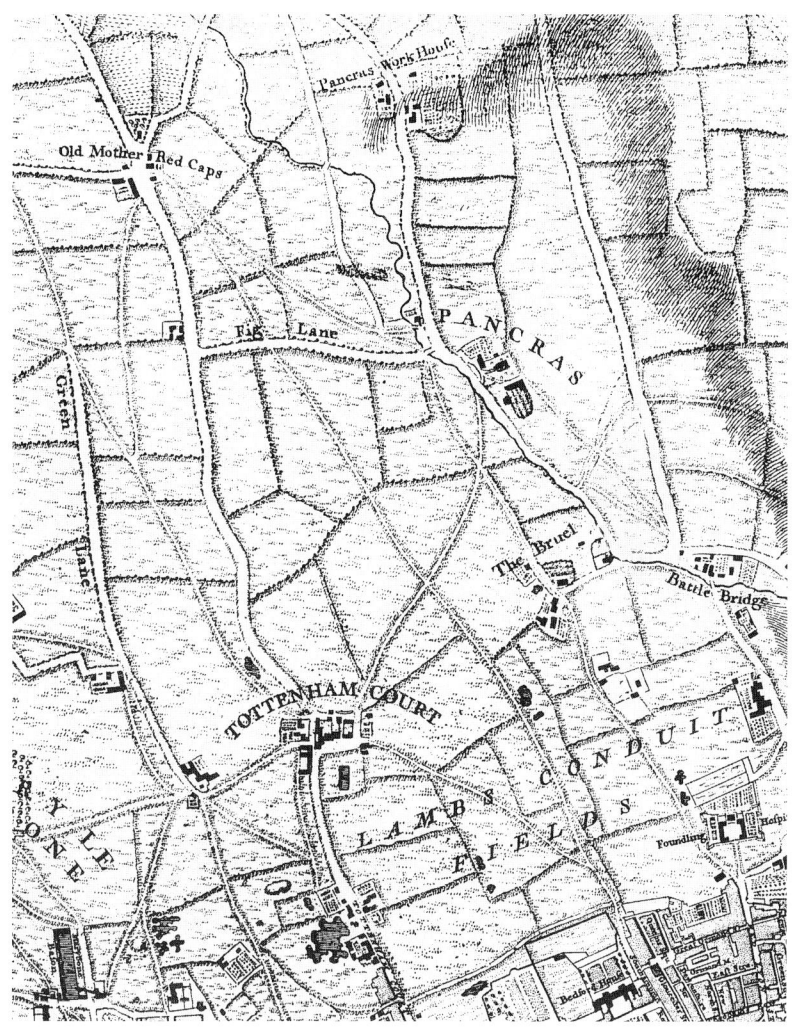

his action against the Regent's Canal Company, but just what game was he playing? His actions – especially during the battles of 1815 – caused suspension of the work. The Company was permitted to raise an extra £200,000 by an Act of 1816, but it got a miserable response from an appeal for further subscriptions. The canal was saved by a loan from the government of £200,000 for one of the first job-creation schemes set up by the Poor Employment Act of 1817.

If he was connected with the company, it is difficult to see how Agar helped it. As Spence (1961) notes, the canal was a failure as a speculation: it did not pay its first dividend until 1829, and then only 12s. 6d. on each £100 share, since it had to settle its debts to the Treasury first.

But a better picture of Agar emerges elsewhere. He clearly took an interest in local affairs. He is listed as one of the founding members of the Select (or closed) Vestry in the St Pancras Vestry Act of 1819, and later that year was nominated, but did not get sufficient votes, to sit on the 40-strong Board of Directors of the Poor. King recalls his "accustomed generosity" when he shows him entertaining in the grounds of Elm Lodge (Fig.4).

Elm Lodge

William Agar built Elm Lodge for himself and his wife Louisa, niece of the Earl of Shrewsbury. A lease of 1789 (Newcombe to Richardson and Harrison, HC BI 41) refers to "a messuage or mansion house with barn and about 4 bays of building" but other references make it clear that this house had long been ruinous. A large-scale map of the parish in 1804 shows no buildings whatever on the site ('Six Acres Field'). Agar built the house shortly after he purchased the estate; drawings of the house (Fig.5), with its rounded bays on the entrance front, confirm that it was a late Georgian building. Elm Lodge was surrounded by a park full of mulberry trees, and a line of tall poplars fringed the grounds as far south as the new St Pancras Workhouse.

Morrell (1935:24) states that in 1811 Agar's lands were assessed as prebendal land at £504, but Agar appealed because the rent was much less and the land area had been reduced by that occupied by St Pancras Workhouse. He said the estate was 72 acres, 3 roods and 26 perches. On 2 March 1816 the prebendary William Beloe (died 1817) formally leased the manor to Agar, most of which was already in his occupation. The Agar family took out two further leases. In 1822 William leased West Acres and Middle Field, and on 9 April 1839 his widow Louisa took out another lease on the grounds surrounding Elm Lodge.

A map of the parliamentary borough of St Marylebone in 1834 (Fig.6) shows the extent of buildings on the manor, confined to the area around St Pancras Workhouse and St Pancras Old Church, with Elm Lodge and its gardens to the north. A footpath leads over the Skew Bridge (also called Oblique Bridge) across the Regent's Canal which bisects the area. This footpath was to form the line of Cambridge Street and Salisbury Street – the main thoroughfare of Agar Town.

Fig. 5 Elm Lodge, coloured drawing by unknown artist (Camden Local Studies Library)

Fig. 6 Map of part of the Parliamentary Borough of St Marylebone, from the Survey of 1834. The faint hatching is original, and denotes agricultural land. 19, the part of the original prebendal manor by this time owned by St Bartholomew's Hospital. 17, the Brewer's Company estate. (Camden Local Studies Library)

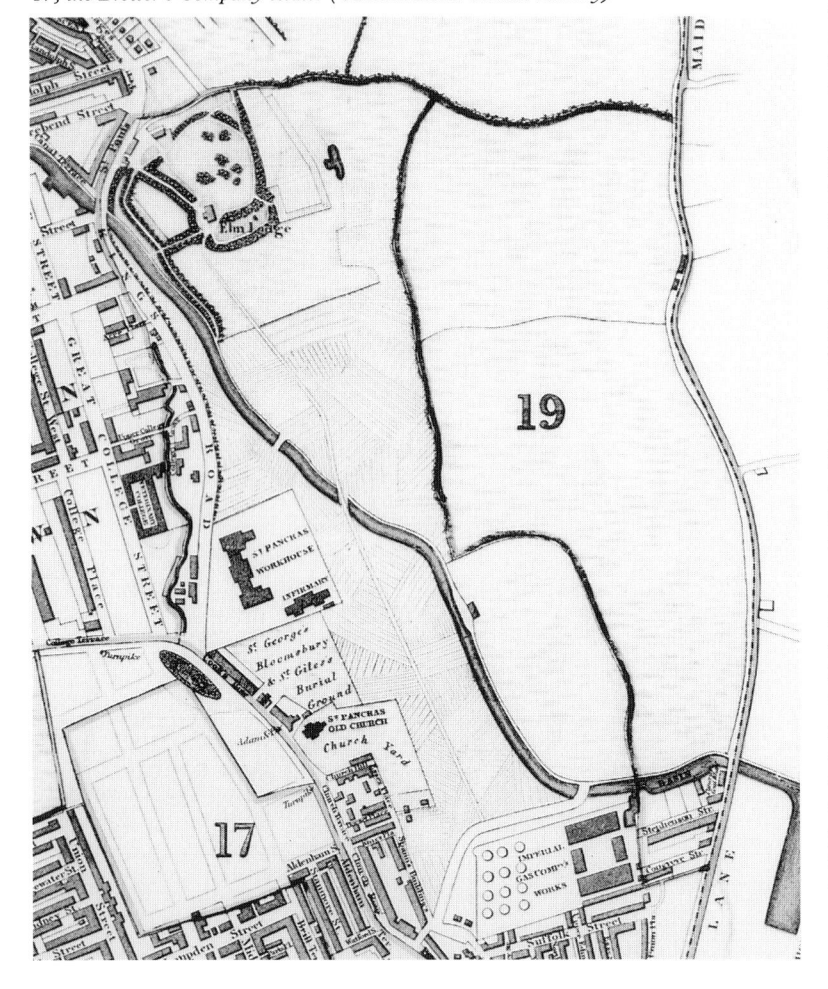

3: Working-class housing in early Victorian London

IN CONSIDERING the development of Agar Town one must not lose sight of the appalling conditions in which most Londoners lived. The working class was effectively trapped in central London (Jones, 1984), because they had to be near their work. Most working-class Londoners were unskilled and their work was mainly seasonal and casual. Suburban rents were far cheaper than those in central London because of lower land values and because builders could evade even rudimentary building controls. But working-class Londoners could not afford to commute. Omnibus fares were too expensive and working men walked to work.

Yet it was becoming increasingly difficult to live in the central area, given the large-scale demolition of lower-class housing from the 1830s on. Large tracts of the City and surrounding districts to the north and east were being converted into warehouses and offices, exacerbating the housing shortage for the working class, already acute because of a spiralling population. When Agar Town was being developed in the 1840s conditions for the working class in London were especially severe. Wages and standards of working conditions were falling, with intense competition between metropolitan trades. Housing conditions deteriorated after the collapse of the house-building boom in 1825. More and more people were becoming paupers. There was intense concern during the 1840s about urban industrial society and the pressures on housing.

These conditions encouraged the growth of slums. New building had rarely been directed at the lower class, so that most of the latter occupied housing which had once accommodated people of substance: it was always cheaper to subdivide than to build. The worst slums were in what were formerly the best houses, lacking ready access to water and means of heating, and often severely overcrowded. They stood amidst accumulations of refuse, offal from slaughterhouses and household manure, even though this was profitable to vestries because it could be sold off to farmers.

The very lowest weekly rents – the Irish in Holborn in 1840 were paying 1s. to 1s.6d – bought one room, probably without a sink or grate; 2s.6d to 4s.6d bought one or two rooms with access to a shared water tap and privy, while 5s. could buy two rooms in a model dwelling. Living in rooms was the norm for the majority of the working-class – a rent of 4s. was about the maximum that most labourers on wages of 15s. to 20s. a week could afford. Skilled artisans might be able to rent a terraced house, but this was the upper limit of working-class respectability. Poorer people might live more or less permanently in common lodging houses intended as minimal temporary accommodation. Hole (1866) stressed the powerlessness of the working class who could not move from the centre, were compelled to take houses near their work and paid a large proportion of their income on rent. "The most respectable of the labouring classes who though earning high wages were pauperised by the expenses of the sickness brought on them by these dwellings" (Hole, 1866:50) and were thus isolated from the "beneficial moral influence of the middle class" (Hole, 1866:67).

However, not all overcrowded and slum property was to be found in tenements in central London. On the fringes of the central area but within walking distance of their place of work, labourers and others might find accommodation in recent but shoddily built houses in low-lying areas often close to noxious factories – backwaters which could not attract any other class. Burnett suggests that among speculative builders jerry-building was very common, because it would be unrealistic to expect traditional small-scale builders, in a technologically backward industry not mechanised until after 1850, to be concerned with proper ventilation, sewage or water supplies unless compelled (Burnett, 1986:71). Building standards and planning requirements did not begin to bite until after the mid-century. Builders and their sub-contractors skimped on materials and structures, and jerry-built houses tended to turn into slums. Dyos wrote "it was sometimes possible to run through the complete declension from meadow to slum in a single generation, or even less" (1982:141).

4: The image of Agar Town

Modern references to Agar Town

DYOS may have had Agar Town in mind, and Gillian Tindall (1980:127) certainly makes the connection. Gaskell (1990:59) calls it a shanty town which had a justifiable reputation within a decade since the houses were little more than huts made from bricks and rubbish. Coppock and Prince go further by saying that the buildings of Agar Town were "slums from the day they were first occupied" (1964:112), inhabited by washerwomen and dustmen. Kellett (1969) stresses its location, which he calls a paralysed wedge sandwiched between King's Cross and Euston, an example of makeshift inner suburbs caused by the rapid growth of urban population creating a large class unable to pay for anything better. Railways increased the stream of dispossessed, leading to more overcrowding and cramped inner districts. "Inner districts intersected by the railways were fixed in dereliction" (Kellett, 1969:343).

However, King's Cross station was not built until more than 10 years after Agar Town was begun. Most modern references to Agar Town, which are cursory and sparse, contain factual inaccuracies. For example, Best writes of ghastly new-built slums like "Agar's Town [sic]...which crawled out of the mud between the Euston Road and the Regent's Park Canal about 1810, and was obliterated by St Pancras station fifty years later" (1979:49). Agar Town was in fact begun in 1840, developed mainly north of the canal and was not the site of St Pancras Station but its approach.

But worse are writers on slums who lump Agar Town together with older areas like Jacob's Island or St Giles. Wohl talks of "hell holes, utterly fantastic in their labyrinthine streets and decrepit structures" (1979:28) and later "only when the full horror of conditions in areas like Agar Town or St Giles is grasped can one appreciate the enthusiasm with which their destruction was greeted" (1979:39).

I aim to show that this simply will

Fig. 7 Agar Town as depicted in The Builder, 8 Oct 1853 (Camden Local Studies Library)

not do. What all modern historians have done in dealing with Agar Town is to recycle uncritically contemporary descriptions about the area. These should not be taken at face value.

Contemporary references to Agar Town

In The Kentish Town Roll (a panorama of the road from St Pancras Old Church to Kentish Town, drawn in the late 1840s but recalling a period earlier in the century) Mr King shows the seat of Counsellor Agar (Fig.4) and 'the immense number of poplars' which shaded the road as far as his property extended. But he adds "since then they have all been cut down and two- and four-roomed cottages have been built by Working Men at a ground rent, on the road side, payable weekly or monthly. The Leases terminate at the end of 21 years, which have brought together such a variety of Poor to the area known as Agar Town extending to the Gas Works in Maiden Lane [sic!] as to make it a Second Saint Giles, it being very hazardous for any respectable person to pass or repass without insult, or annoyance, as that locality received most of the refuse which the forming of New Oxford Street swept away to improve that previous impure district" (Survey of London, XIX:61).

King was a local man, clearly resentful of the rapid change in the area. He introduces the idea that many of the inhabitants of Agar Town are from St Giles. This was taken up in an influential article (reproduced in Annex 1, p.29) in Charles Dickens' *Household Words*, 1851, p.652. Written by W. Thomas (and not Dickens as several modern historians believe) this states that "the inhabitants exhibit a genuine Irish apathy". The article relates the imaginary tale of a Manchester man seeking a residence in London who gets a favourable but false picture of Agar Town from the map. When he gets there he finds the roads unmade, created between rows of houses opposite each other and churned into paste by carts from brickfields. There are no sewers – people throw everything out in front and there it stays; doors are blocked up with mud, and by heaps of ashes, oyster shells and decayed vegetables. Every tenant has his own lease of land and there is a great variety in the buildings: dog kennels, cow sheds, watch boxes. Every garden has its nuisance: dung heaps, cinder heaps, whelk and winkle shells from costermongers.

This 'Dickens' article generated a good deal of interest in the sanitary condition of Agar Town. In June 1851 a Board of Health report said the district was "one of the most neglected in the metropolis. Its roads made one think of some decayed country town", drawing the conclusion that something must be done "to remedy those evils which are caused by the present unnatural state of society, and by the crowding together of a rapidly increasing population in cities and towns" (PP, 1851, XXIII:33). Papers which promoted housing reform, such as *The Builder*, turned their attention to Agar Town. The *Builder*'s leading article on cholera and sanitation, 8 October 1853, stated:

"No words would be too strong to describe the miserable conditions of this disgraceful location. The houses have been planted here without any thought of drainage, or of any other arrangement necessary for health: it is as ill considered as some of the extempore towns in the neighbourhood of the gold diggings".

Fever was said to be raging, and the medical attendant was said to feel that there was no use in giving medicine in conditions which included open cesspools and water in a black poisonous stream beneath floor boards. Snails, spiders and vermin were plentiful. There was a daily overflow of water, yet on Sundays Agar Town was 'dry' (ie there was no piped water). "Can it be necessary to say anything more to show how much interference is needed in this miserable district?" (*The Builder*, 8 Oct 1853). The drawing which accompanied this article is shown in Figure 7.

Canon Dale, the Vicar of St Pancras, in evidence to the House of Lords Committee on Spiritual Destitution in 1858, said that the district "is one of extreme and almost unmitigated poverty", with its houses "more fitted for the occupation of wild beasts than for human beings" (Morrell, 1935:37), while in 1861 Hollingshead stated that Agar Town, "built on a swamp, and running down to the canal in every stage of dirt and decay" (1861:9), was a "St Giles really in the fields – a collection of the very lowest order of labourers' cottages... a Dorsetshire under our very walls" (1861:132) and a "house of call for the workhouse" (1861:156). He wrote that half of the houses were cottages or huts standing in black yards. Most had a ground floor only. Some rooms had no doors, others no windows, in others the garden walls had rotted away. Water was kept in holes. Dustbins were unknown in Cambridge Crescent, and public privies were rare. The tiles of these huts were broken off. They had filthy interiors, and outside, sole-skins were hung on clothes lines. Children were barefoot and ragged, yet donkeys roamed about, as well housed as their masters.

The validity of these accounts will be considered below, but on the basis of this picture of Agar Town it is hardly surprising that its demolition in 1866 was not regretted. Most commentators could state categorically that the action of the Midland Railway Company was not only justified but laudable. Williams, in his *History of the Midland Railway* (1874), is typical. Agar Town was "a very 'abomination of desolation'. In its centre was what was named Belle Isle [another error], a dreary unsavoury locality, abandoned to mountains of refuse.... At the broken windows and doors of mutilated houses canaries still sang and dogs lay sleeping in the sun to remind one of the vast colonies of bird and dog fanciers who formerly made their abode here; and from these dwellings wretched creatures came, in rags and dirt, and searched amid the far extending refuse for the filthy treasure by the aid of which they eked out a miserable livelihood; while over the neighbourhood the gas works poured their mephitic vapours and the canal gave forth its rheumatic dampness, extracting in return some of the more poisonous ingredients from the atmosphere and spreading them upon the surface of the water in a thick scum of various and ominous hues. Such was Agar Town before the Midland came" (in Coppock & Prince, 1964:127).

5: Agar Town – a slum?

What makes for a slum?

THERE is general agreement on what made for slum districts. Slums were usually found in low-lying and poorly drained areas, and were isolated, cut off physically, with no through traffic. The barrier effect of railways also helped to foster slum development, as did proximity to factories, gasworks, open sewers and other sources of noxious smells. And lastly there were structural features, such as buildings skimped or built on inadequately settled 'made ground' and repairs ignored. "They all acted as tourniquets applied for too long, and below them a gangrene inevitably set in" (Dyos & Wolff, 1973:364).

How many of these factors applied to Agar Town?

Location

Agar Town was developed on the pasture land of the prebendal manor of St Pancras. This is a zone of uneven clay between the high ridge of Highgate and Hampstead and the flat, well-drained gravel terrace on which 18th-century developments like Marylebone had taken place. The article in *Household Words* states that the land was well situated, for the most part high, and could be adapted for the erection of small tenements for working men. It was not "a swamp" as Hollingshead suggested. However, on the London clay special precautions needed to be taken in laying foundations and draining to prevent deterioration. Contemporary accounts suggest that this was not done.

An isolated area?

Agar's estate did have some advantages – in 1840 it was open both to the north as far as the road from Camden Town to Tottenham, and to the east as far as Maiden Lane (present-day York Way). Kellett's description of the area as a paralysed wedge is inaccurate. It was only from 1850 hemmed in to the north by the North London line and to the east by the GNR goods yard and the line into King's Cross Station which opened in 1851. To the west it was fringed by the main route from the City to Camden and Kentish Towns. Toll gates along this turnpiked road must have kept the traffic down. After they were removed in 1864, the Vestry minutes (VM, 10 May 1865) note a large increase in traffic, although this was also due to completion of the Midland Railway stores in northern Agar Town. The general picture is not of a particularly isolated area.

Proximity to industry

Miller in 1874 wrongly stated that Belle Isle – the home of refuse, knackers' yards and manure-making factories

Fig. 8   St Pancras Old Church and its burial ground (from the Kentish Town Roll, see Fig. 4)

and other chemical works – was at the centre of Agar Town. Belle Isle was in fact in Maiden Lane, and Agar Town did not stretch so far. The prevailing winds were westerly, but a sickening smell may have pervaded the area if they changed direction. A leading article in *The Metropolitan* (13 September 1856) states that "the nuisance makers of Belle Isle are still permitted to affect their neighbours with nausea, sickness, diarrhoea, dysentery and cholera to any extent they please for their own private advantage". It says that the pungent fumes could cause sneezing and runny eyes a mile off and it feared that Agar Town might lose its infant population from scarlatina.

The canal about which Agar Town developed may have been polluted by industrial effluent from the works of the Imperial Gas, Light and Coke Company immediately to the south. "The most offensive and pestilential nuisances in London are its gasworks" (*The Builder*, 6 May 1854). Although Agar Town was primarily residential, the canal encouraged some small-scale industrial development along its banks, backing Cambridge Street. In the 1850s these included Starkey's, the nightmen's yard, a "monster nuisance which impregnates the atmosphere for miles around nightly with the most noxious effluvia arising from the burning of all sorts of filth and refuse" (*The Builder*, 14 Oct 1854).

The burial grounds

The southern area of Agar Town abutted on two burial grounds, one ancient, one modern, but both packed with bodies. In the burial ground of St Pancras Old Church (Fig.8) there were nearly 27,000 burials in the 20 years to 1847. *The Builder* in December 1853 noted that fungus grew in St Pancras Old Church because it was in the centre of so much human decomposition. Indeed, the ground around was raised several feet by the accumulation of bodies. Poisonous gases, diluted by the atmosphere, were said to get into surrounding houses. After the closure of the burial ground in 1854 the Medical Officer of Health reported that it was being used as a rubbish tip (VM, 7 Aug 1856).

Even worse was the adjoining St Giles burial ground, founded in 1803, between St Pancras Old Church and the workhouse. Similar numbers were buried here – 10,000 between 1843 and 1845 alone and 3,000 in 6 months during the 1849 cholera epidemic. The stench was said to be appalling, and there were frequent complaints of body snatching and body burning to make more space. This led to a special parliamentary enquiry in 1850 to investigate 'alleged revolting practices'. A pall of smoke and smell was found to be hanging over the burial ground.

An inevitable slum?

The surroundings of St Pancras manor would not have encouraged middle-class development, but in 1840 it still retained an open aspect, and the noxious smells from the gasworks, the burial grounds and most notably from Belle Isle may have been no more than an irritant. Indeed, the solidly middle-class district of Camden New Town (the area around Camden Square), immediately to the north of Agar Town and even closer to the factories of Belle Isle, was being laid out in the 1840s and 1850s. This was built on the same band of uneven clay.

None of the factors so far discussed would mean that slum development was inevitable. We need to explore the way housing was developed, to see what controls existed, whether the area was planned, and whether repairs were carried out if we are to decide whether Agar Town deserved the reputation housing reformers gave it.

6: The development of Agar Town

Role of the Agar family

WHEN he died in 1838 William Agar left all his property to his wife Louisa to hold for his two children, William Talbot Agar and Louisa Agar the Younger. His will, dated 9 September 1834 and proved on 8 December 1838, authorised his wife to grant any leases of any parts of his estates for any terms not exceeding 21 years for the best rents that could reasonably be had without taking any fine or forfeit for granting such leases (B/NTG/1268 & Middx Reg 1843/6/3).

Hollingshead (1861:131) suggests that this was a deliberate act of bad faith by Agar, who, he claims, 25 years before expiry of his lease had applied unsuccessfully to the Ecclesiastical Commissioners for a long lease in anticipation of railway development and then, to spite the landlord, had let the land off to the lowest class. A very colourful account, but the Ecclesiastical Commissioners did not become owners of the land until 1847, and William Agar himself died before any of the land was let. More importantly, by two statutes of Elizabeth I leases of church lands were limited to 21 years or 3 lives. The *Household Words* article noted that the present owners held the land for a term of 3 lives, with power to lease for periods of not more than 21 years.

Louisa Agar, assisted by her two adult children, started to let the land in 1840 (B/NTG/1273), no doubt conscious that they were more likely to get a higher return by leasing land for building than using it for agriculture. The family was soon to get well over £70 per acre from ground rents (see Annex 2, p.31).

Besides the generally undesirable location, 21-year leases were a further factor inhibiting a good class of development. The Agar family made matters worse by letting off the land in very small plots. Yet conditions were attached to the leases, for example for drainage and repair, and there is evidence of concern that houses on prominent sites or main thoroughfares had some degree of regularity.

The agreements reached were rarely in the form of formal indentures. Beames says that Agar Town was settled illegally, containing "a squalid population, originally a band of settlers, who seem, as they would say in America, to have squatted there, and now it is almost impossible to remove them" (1852:15). This is utter nonsense. All the land was let legally by the Agar family in the form of written agreements.

By mid-1842 the Agar family had leased 40 of their 72 acres, and by 1844 most of the estate other than the fairly extensive grounds near Elm Lodge was let. They continued to let portions for building until 1847, when the Ecclesiastical Commissioners became the freeholder following the death of the last prebendary of St Pancras, Arthur Robinson Chauvel, on 21 January. The change of owner did not prevent the Agar family from disposing of parts of the estate as they saw fit. In April 1849 they granted a strip of land of roughly 4 acres running across the northern part of their estate, forming part of the garden land and pleasure ground of Elm Lodge itself, to the East and West India Docks and Birmingham Junction Railway Company (now the North London line) for £5,000 (Middx Reg 1850/4/421). In 1850 they granted 8 acres on the east side of the canal to the GNR (Middx Reg 1853/13/438).

It is often said that the Agars were ejected because of bad management, but they maintained a close interest in Agar Town throughout the 1850s. On 13 November 1851 they drew up articles of agreement with the Ecclesiastical Commissioners that from midsummer 1850 for a term of 80 years they should receive from the rents and profits of the estate at least £1,200 per annum. In return the Agar family agreed to set aside the £5,000 they had received from the East and West India Docks and Birmingham Junction Railway Company to form a fund for the improvement of Agar Town. These arrangements were sufficiently well known at the time for Canon Dale to explain them in 1858 to the House of Lords Committee on Spiritual Destitution (PP, 1857-8, IX: 201).

These articles of agreement were drawn up into a formal indenture in 1853 (Middx Reg 1856/8/66) which mentioned that Louisa Agar the Elder was granted the mansion house and grounds provided she continued to live there. She and her two children were at least nominally living in Elm Lodge in 1853 but the house must have become increasingly marooned, overshadowed by the viaduct of what became the North London Railway and by roads being made throughout the 1850s into what were once Agar Fields, which had separated the house from Agar Town. Louisa Agar the Younger was still there on the 1861 census.

In 1860 the Agar family relinquished all interest in the estate for a sum which is unfortunately not specified in the records (Middx Reg 1860/6/996).

Building development

There would have been no Agar Town but for the Agar family's decision to lease the land. But it was the builders who determined the character of the area. Miller wrote that the tenements were run up by anyone disposed to take the ground. "Many were mere hovels erected by journeymen bricklayers and carpenters on Sundays and in other spare time, and were inhabited before the ground flooring was laid" (1874:54). By considering the development of Agar Town we can establish that "Agar Town was an effort by working men to solve the housing problem for themselves" (Sinclair, 1938:60).

At the time it was very easy to run up small houses. Dorothy George quotes an account of 1834 which showed how journeymen earning 20s. to 30s. a week were able to invest money in building cottages, using an old method:

"A builder makes up the carcass, the house just being tiled in. He then lets them for an additional ground rent to mechanics, carpenters, bricklayers and plasterers. He will give them a hundred of deals and a proportionate quality of lime to begin with. The carpenter then agrees with the bricklayer and plasterer that each shall do the work of the other, and with their reciprocal labour and their savings they finish the house" (1965:90).

Such were building clubs, where groups of tradesmen cooperated to build their own houses. Other means of finance included building societies. In the 1840s there were numerous terminating societies, with a fixed number of members who paid contributions for an agreed period (say 10 years) until all had taken loans and paid them off. Clerks and artisans made most use of terminating societies; working-class members had to be good and regular earners.

There were builders who took several leases in Agar Town, and developed a number of dwellings for sale. There were also those who ran up a few cottages and lived in one themselves, collecting the rent from others. But equally there were a large number of leases taken by working men who built homes for themselves. This will become clearer from a chronological description of the growth of Agar Town and a study in depth of one particular area.

The growth of Agar Town

The earliest developments were along King's Road (Agar Cottages) and in the south. The latter were first described on the 1841 census as "cottages near or opposite Spann's Buildings". Detailed papers survive for the 21-year leases on plots in York Place and Canterbury Place, but the Vestry minutes show that the other parts of Agar Town were developed in same way.

By September 1841 the first streets were named – Cambridge Crescent, Oxford Crescent, Oxford Place, Oxford Street, Oxford Terrace. The street names of Agar Town were probably suggested by the fact this was church land, hence Winchester Street, Canterbury Place, York Place, Durham Street.

Cambridge Street, because it backed onto the canal, was industrial from early on, with timber yards and sawmills. Darke's dust yard was listed there as early as 1842. There is, however, no evidence of industry in any other part of Agar Town.

All this early development took place south of the canal. Development north of the canal commenced in 1844 with Salisbury Street, Salisbury Crescent and Winchester Street, all begun on 21- year leases. For example, Henry Freeth, silversmith of Salisbury Street, took out a lease of 21 years from 21 March 1844 on a plot of land 34 ft by 70 ft on which he built two houses. He was financed by a mortgage by what appeared to be a local terminating building society in Clerkenwell.

By 1847 the built-up area of Agar Town was more or less complete until the extensions and improvements of the 1850s. This can be seen in the 1849 parish map (Fig.9) which shows the proposed line of what is now the North London Railway to the north

Fig. 9   Map of St Pancras Parish, 1849 (courtesy of Greater London Record Office)

(perilously close to Elm Lodge, while Agar Town is well away from it). Figure 10 shows a slightly later view of the edge of the Agar Town estate and the St Pancras Workhouse, from the north. From 1855 there were new developments, different in kind from those of the 1840s, in northern Agar Town. The builders involved – the Bareham brothers and Thomas J Bolton – were large-scale operators, who took out 99-year leases from the Ecclesiastical Commissioners and sold on as soon as the houses were completed. Bareham developed houses, all at £20 rateable value, in Durham Terrace in September 1855 and in 1856 began Kingston and Bolton Streets. Bolton played an important role in the extensions of Agar Town in the 1850s, taking leases of large tracts of land in the former Agar Fields.

Agar Town was at its fullest extent by 1860, but by then the Ecclesiastical Commissioners had already sold the freehold of the estate to the Midland Railway Company, in anticipation of its destruction.

Housing types

There was a range of housing in Agar Town. That of the 1850s was fairly typical suburban development, while that developed under 21-year leases in the 1840s and often the result of self-help was rather more individual cottage development. There is evidence that such housing took some time to build, probably because it was constructed in spare time, especially on Sundays (HC BI 35). The London City Mission Magazine, Nov 1846, stated that "at the east end of Cambridge Street just by the Gasworks were seen about 6 men laying the foundation of 2 dwellings, and a number looking on. By the next day these residences had been reared several feet. During the whole of the ensuing week nothing was done". Work then started again the following Sunday.

Rateable values can shed some light on the type of properties built. Gavin in 1850 wrote that in London the "average rated rental of houses inhabited by the labouring classes is under £8" (1850:16). At that time values in Agar Town ranged from about £5 in Cambridge Crescent, through £12 in Durham Street and £16 in Oxford Street to £16 or £18 in Winchester Terrace (then facing open fields, although the GNR goods yard had been sanctioned).

Houses in Winchester Terrace rated at £18 p.a. were being rented at 8s. a week in July 1847, houses in Oxford Street (nos. 6-9) rated at £16 were let at 5s. 6d in June 1849. Such rents would have been aimed at artisans. Rating appeals in 1845 yield some useful information on rents being charged. At the lowest end of the scale were the cottages in Cambridge Crescent. Charles Green, landlord of 1-3 Cambridge Crescent, each rated at £12, asked to 'compound' them at just £4 each because the tenements had only one room and would not command the rental charge, namely 2s. 6d a week. [Compounding became increasingly common in Agar Town from the mid 1840s. An Act (59 Geo III, c.39) allowed owners of tenements let at a yearly rate not exceeding £20 p.a. or payable at periods less than quarterly to compound. Owners incorporated rates into rent. Compounding meant reductions in rates of sometimes as much as 50% but the saving was to the landlord, not the tenant.] Hezekiah Bell let the nearby 30 Upper Cambridge Street 'consisting of two rooms and a washhouse' at £10 p.a. or 5s. a week. In 1851 the *Household Words* article cited a respectable mechanic paying 6s. a week for his damp hut of two rooms with its boards laid upon the ground.

The wide range of housing is corroborated by the most detailed map of Agar Town, that deposited by the Midland Railway Company in 1863. Salisbury Crescent has some very irregularly shaped cottages running down to the canal, while round the corner in Winchester Terrace there is regular terraced housing. The largest houses are the most recent: St George's Terrace along Cambridge Street East Side, where each house had a rateable value of £24 16s 8d, a 16-ft frontage and 81-ft depth.

Improvements

By 1860 Agar Town was paved and lit, but for many years this was not the case. The Agar Town estate was not the responsibility of a Paving Commission. As early as 14 September 1840 the Vestry had appointed a Committee to consider which areas in the parish, including Agar Town, needed paving and lighting. But a decade

Fig.10 St Pancras Workhouse and the edge of the Agar Town estate, drawn by Henry Guest RA (a Camden Town resident) in the 1850s (courtesy of Greater London Record Office)

later the Vestry minutes show that none of the roads there were paved, and other than the new streets in the north they were still largely unpaved on 14 July 1858, when estimates for paving roads and footways were recorded. Hollingshead (1861) noted that when he had visited in 1851 the roads were simply mud-filled ditches and the footpaths were raised earth-banks. A Sanitary Committee report presented to the Vestry on 16 October 1856 stated that the "roads through Agar Town are in a condition which baffles description.... mud in many places lies knee deep". In bad weather and in winter the roads were said to be impassable.

There were active efforts to improve Agar Town during the 1850s. Some of the earliest properties were pulled down. Parts of Oxford Crescent, Oxford Place and Oxford Street were demolished between September 1853 and September 1854, although this was mainly in preparation for a road to connect up with Queen's Road in Camden New Town. The Ecclesiastical Commissioners asked the Vestry to undertake the foundations of this road because they considered they had only a limited interest in the property, whereas the Vestry thought this was for the owners of Agar Town. A newspaper report of 1853 (HC BI 42) records their meeting. The Ecclesiastical Commissioners had written to lessees on 28 July to offer to lay down drains into the main sewer in Cambridge Street – constructed at "great expense" by them – and to defray half the expense if the lessees met the balance. There had been not one reply. The Vestry said it was determined to improve Agar Town under powers vested by the Board of Health, to purify defective houses, to cleanse drains and ditches and to remove nuisances. At the meeting it was confirmed that there were covenants in the leases for repair and insurance, which the Vestry said it was prepared to enforce by wholesale evictions. There is nothing to suggest that this happened.

Morrell (1935) states without giving any detail that the Ecclesiastical Commissioners together with the Vicar Canon Dale and the Agar family mitigated the evils of the area and drew up plans to erect a better neighbourhood. Canon Dale in his 1858 evidence to the House of Lords Committee on Spiritual Destitution said that "the Ecclesiastical Commissioners had done a great deal during the past twelve months towards the improvement of the district ... which is now undergoing a most favourable change" and that "Agar Town, formerly the most destitute district in the parish, both temporally and spiritually, is very much improved". Chalk, Secretary to the Ecclesiastical Commissioners, puffing their work to the Lords Committee, said that Agar Town had been "one of the most disgraceful properties to be found anywhere. Since the Commissioners acquired possession of it it has greatly improved; but it must be a work of time to render it thoroughly respectable" (PP, 1857-8, IX:507).

The Ecclesiastical Commissioners were not quite so altruistic as this appears. The improvements to paving and lighting were undertaken using the fund set aside some years before by the Agar family and with money lent at interest to the Vestry after many years of wrangling about which roads were public and which private. The improvements were clearly designed to increase the value of the estate. And in *The Builder*, 22 October 1853, an inhabitant of Agar Town complained that the Ecclesiastical Commissioners, who he claimed received many thousands annually for all the ground, "are the really blameable parties for the want of drainage". He felt they should provide a proper sewer since a 4-inch main choked for four months was all they had. Hollingshead in 1861 said it was the Vestry that had provided lamps and pavements in defiance of the Ecclesiastical Commissioners "who could never be brought to any sense of their public duty" (1861:132).

But the Vestry had not exactly rushed to improve matters either. They did seek powers from Parliament to pave areas outside those covered by the Paving Commissioners, but their St Pancras (Consolidation of Paving Boards) Bill had been rejected by the House of Lords in August 1851 and subsequently they opposed calls from ratepayers to reopen the issue. It was not until the Ecclesiastical Commissioners threatened legal action if the main streets of Agar Town were not properly lit that the Vestry took action. An agreement was drawn up between them in January 1857 (VM, 7 Nov 1860) that in return for a loan of £1,800 with interest the Vestry would put lighting in place at once.

A lighting rate for Agar Town householders was introduced immediately, but lighting itself took longer. There were petitions from disgruntled ratepayers in February 1857, but it was October before the surveyor presented a lighting plan for the estate. Lighting was introduced soon after but not to the satisfaction of the Ecclesiastical Commissioners, who were threatening legal action again on 7 July 1858.

By this time the Vestry was seeking estimates for making up the roads, but on 4 May 1859 the Vestry claimed to a deputation from ratepayers that it was still awaiting receipt of the loan! The Vestry did pave all roads on the Estate during 1860 and then set an improvement rate to recoup their expenditure. The Commissioners gave notice of appeal against the imposition of this special rate, which they considered an interference with their own property. By this time they had different plans for Agar Town. They told the Vestry that it had thrown money away in paving their 'private streets'. They would pay the £536 the Vestry had spent on those streets south of the canal if the Vestry recognised that these were private roads, since the Ecclesiastical Commissioners intended "their being done away with altogether".

A Case Study: York Place and Canterbury Place

A look in greater depth at one area will bring out some of the issues so far discussed.

The southern portions of Agar's land were amongst the first to be developed. Immediately north of the gasworks, the land between Spann's Buildings and the canal was parcelled out in small plots on 21-year leases from early 1840. A block of land of just under an acre, first known as Spann's Buildings East Side and by May 1842 as York Place and Canterbury Place, can be studied in some detail because of records remaining in the Greater London Record Office. These records show how working men built for themselves.

The land was let out in narrow strips which abutted a ditch which bisected the area from north to south. A typical plot was 32 ft by 72 ft. Most of the earliest agreements were made in May 1840. These were recorded simply on scraps of paper but signed by Mrs Agar and by the lessee and invariably witnessed by William Talbot Agar. Later the agreements were more formally drawn up as full indentures, signed and sealed, although the cost of this appears to have been borne by the lessee.

Both in the simple agreements and the more formal leases lists of conditions were attached which belie the idea that there was no structure to the development of Agar Town. Within a specified period – usually 12 months – the lessee was usually expected to build one or more houses, depending on the size of the plot. Houses were nearly always to be of two rooms, but none of the rooms was to be less than 120 square ft, or 10 ft by 12 ft, nor less than 8 ft in height. The flooring had to be 12 or more inches from the surface of the ground. The area around the plot had to be fenced and both fence and house kept in good repair. Mrs Agar retained the right to inspect the premises on a regular basis and expected the house to be given two coats of oil paint once every 4 years and kept in good repair. There was to be no building or keeping of animals (pigs were specifically prohibited) which might be a nuisance to the area, although on some agreements 'animal keeping' has been crossed out in pencil. The ground rent had to be paid quarterly and if not paid within 3 months of the due date the lease was forfeit. The formal indentures add the proviso that fire insurance 'in some reputable office of insurance' should be taken out; ground rent was still payable in the event of fire.

How far these conditions were enforced (if at all) is debatable. All the houses were duly developed and none of the lessees seem ever to have forfeited their leases. Whether the houses were built to the appropriate specifications cannot be determined. However, a plan of 10-14 Canterbury were very small and almost all were occupied by just one family in 1841 and 1851. Details of construction were unfortunately not given.

The annual ground rents charged varied roughly in relation to the size of the plot from £2 10s to £8, and the Agar family obtained a good return, at a rate of over £76 per acre (see Annex 2). But working men benefited too, by being able to build houses for themselves or to rent. The occupations of the 18 original lessees have not all been recorded but most were employed in the building industry, either as landlord: 2-7 and 9-12 York Place (his brother Hugh Blunt was landlord of 8 and 8a) and 8-11 Canterbury Place. He laid out nearly £500 to acquire the properties, later selling his interest to the Imperial Gas Company in 1860 for £250, not a bad price considering the leases had on average only 18 months to run.

The rents charged in York Place and Canterbury Place suggest that the tenants had to be in fairly well-paid employment. In 1843 the weekly tenants of 10 and 11 Canterbury Place paid 6s. In 1860 the tenants of the

Fig.11 Wesleyan Chapel and Sunday School in Lower Cambridge Street. Henry Guest, 1857 (courtesy of Greater London Record Office)

Place (B/NTG/1269) survives which suggests that at least some of the houses were constructed as planned. The plot was one of the largest, being 64 ft by 72 ft, on which Thomas Vickers Senior of Penton Place, Clerkenwell, carpenter, agreed on 16 March 1842 to build four two-roomed houses within two years. In fact he squeezed in a terrace of five houses. Each house had a room with a fireplace on the ground floor with stairs leading, presumably, to a bedroom over, and a tiny kitchen with a sink. There was an outdoor privy, and both sink and privy were attached by a drain to what is shown on the plan as a drain but must be the open ditch at the back of the plots.

These five houses were rated at £12 p.a., as were nearly all those in York Place and Canterbury Place. Nearly all the leases specified two-roomed houses and the rateable values suggests that they were. Some dwellings had alternative designations, eg Alpha Cottages and Hope Cottages. 'Cottage' may mean they were only of one storey. Certainly the plot size ensured they bricklayers or carpenters. Several continued to live in the buildings they constructed. For example, Edward Manion, an Irish bricklayer and first on the site, lived at Manion's Cottage (16 York Place) until April 1852 when his interest was bought out by his immediate neighbour at Hearne Cottage (Samuel Hearne Le Petit), a solicitor's clerk. Hearne's widow was still living there in 1860 and collecting rent on 16 York Place and 1 Canterbury Place. James Hoyle, journeyman carpenter of Somers Town, and latterly his widow Mary Ann Hoyle lived at their two-roomed Grape Vine Cottage (14 York Place), and she was still paying rates for the property until March 1860, after all the other lessees had sold their interest to the Imperial Gas Company.

Other lessees developed the housing and then rented it out. A handful of the lessees sold their interest in the lease after a few years. John Bannister sold 7 and 8 York Place to the grocer William Blunt in 1843. Over the next 15 years Blunt steadily acquired property in the two streets until he was the major adjoining houses were paying 5s.6d. The range seems to have been between 4s.6d and 6s. for each house that was let. The 1851 census shows that only one dwelling had more than one family living in it, so subletting appears to have been rare.

Like most of Agar Town the streets remained unpaved and unlit until the late 1850s. The cost of paving for York Place for both footways and the road was estimated at £250. From rate records it appears that the street was unlit until late 1859.

Unlike the rest of Agar Town, these two streets did not fall prey to the railways but to the Imperial Gas Company, which bought out Blunt and the other remaining lessees for just over £750 in early 1860. At the end of July 1860 the Vestry's Chief Surveyor reported that the company had put up a hoarding in Canterbury Place to enclose its property. This encroached upon the public thoroughfare and the Vestry considered that the company were indictable. However, it agreed to support the company's application to the quarter sessions to stop up York Place in return for widening the adjoining roads (GLRO, SB 2352). The site was cleared and gas tanks were constructed which in the 1880s were to be surrounded by the impressive gasholders, now listed, that are visible from many adjacent districts and from trains leaving or arriving at King's Cross or St Pancras stations.

Conclusion

The surroundings of Agar Town, the short leases and the absence until 1860 of both paving and lighting could not have made for a good district. But did it deserve its reputation? Gavin (1850) noted that throughout London houses were built near filthy nuisances – open sewers, foul pools, graveyards – and were unfit for human habitation by their very location. "An immense majority of the poor and labouring population live in houses of one room only, or in one room of a 2-, 3- or 4-roomed house" (Gavin, 1850:31) in rooms seldom above 7 ft high, sometimes only 6 ft. Substandard housing for the working class was commonplace. Builders skimped on materials: new houses often collapsed, and the life expectancy of working-class housing was low.

In this general picture conditions in Agar Town were unremarkable. Indeed, rateable values were generally higher than the £8 average; if the covenants in the leases were generally adhered to room sizes were an average 8 ft by 10 ft; and much of Agar Town was built with regular terraced housing. Writers may have focused on some of the smaller, earliest cottage development in low-rated Cambridge Crescent.

Furthermore, writers like Gavin emphasise that in most of London the "houses of the poor are crammed into the smallest possible space" (1850:23). The early housing in Agar Town, while small, was on its own plot of land. Hollingshead (1861) says that one advantage of Agar Town over most districts was that the air was remarkably pure because the spaces between low dwellings were very open. There were no labyrinths of courts between the streets. An impression of this can be gained from the drawing (Fig.11) of the Wesleyan Chapel and Sunday School in Lower Cambridge Street, which can be clearly identified in the 1862 Cassell map (Fig.12). The houses built by working men who took out leases from the Agar family may have been jerry-built, but they were often built for their own occupation. They ensured the retention of gardens and yards in the development for work and for pleasure.

The picture will not, however, be complete until we have examined the people of Agar Town.

Fig.12 Cassell map of 1862 (Camden Local Studies Library) Arrow, the Sunday School in Fig.11

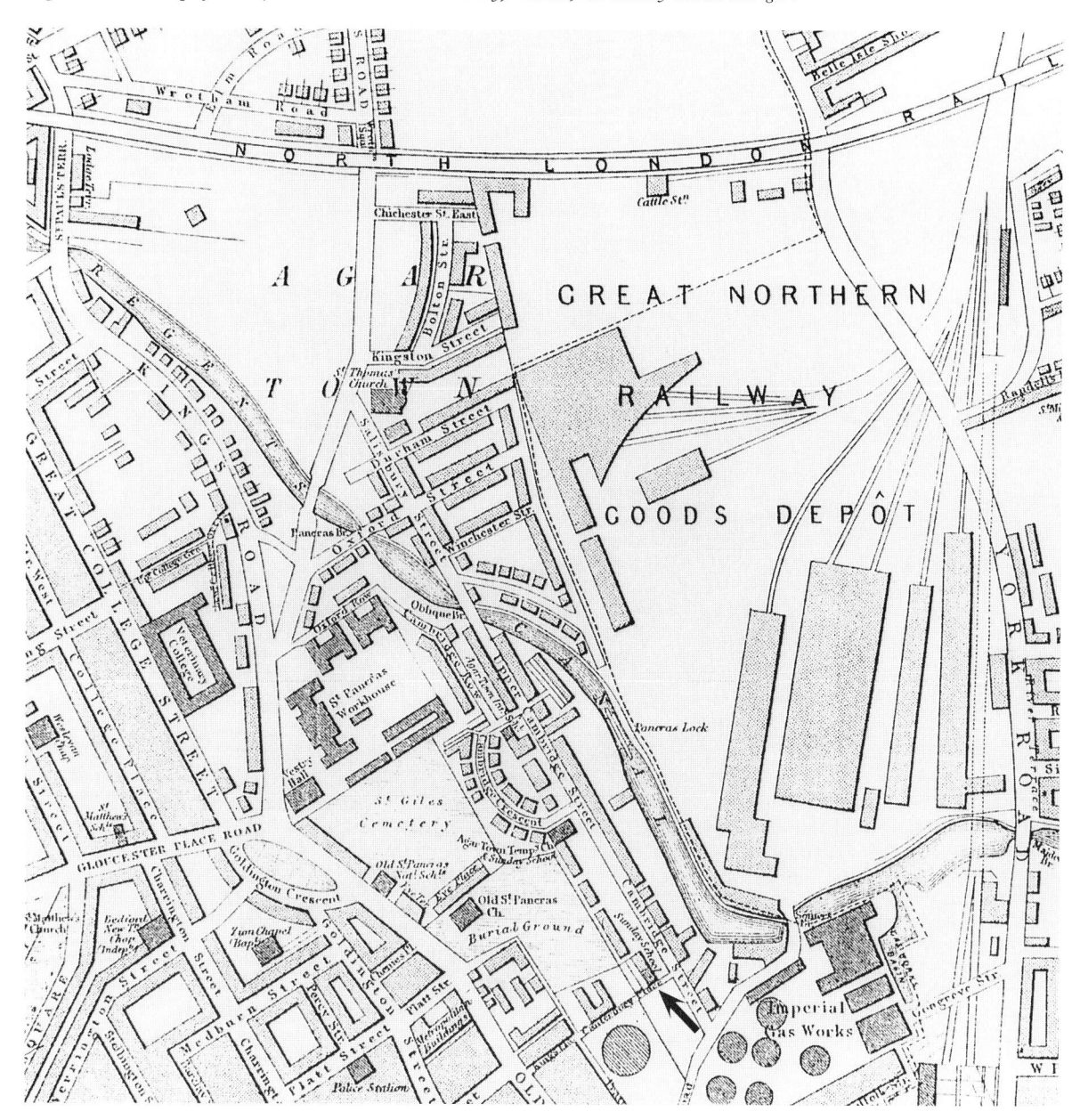

7: The people of Agar Town

Contemporary accounts

AGAR TOWN is usually presented as a notorious slum area crammed with the penniless and the poor Irish of St Giles, some contemporaries do differentiate between inhabitants. The London City Mission Magazine in 1846 found the inhabitants to be a mixture of hard-working mechanics and respectable poor people and those from the lowest grade of society. Towards the east were "not only the ungodly, but the exceedingly depraved, wretched and degraded" (in Morrell, 1935:35). Hollingshead (1861) conceded that in the upper portion of the town near the GNR goods yard lived hard-working mechanics and railwaymen – the houses were not hovels, but like those in railway towns such as Crewe or Wolverton.

Mayne (1993) has identified the recurrent Victorian images of slumland types or urban degenerates. Charity workers visiting slums encountered women most often, because men were at work. The good woman is the one busy mopping. The bad is untidy, cannot budget and gossips too long. The most frequent type is the fallen woman. Foreigners are common, especially the Irish – unskilled, brawling and drunken. The landlord is rapacious. Children swarm, whimper, are neglected and unhealthy and 'must be saved'. A crusade (by police and sanitary authorities) is needed against such heathen territories.

These images can all be found in accounts of life in Agar Town, although there is little which truly brings the place to life. Early and mid-Victorian

Fig.13 *Another view of Agar Town. Henry Guest, 1857 (courtesy of Greater London Record Office)*

whose homes were destroyed when New Oxford Street was formed. Morrell (1935) notes that Mayhew refers to Agar Town being partly occupied by costermongers and by dog and bird fanciers eg hawkers (who caught birds), chickweed and groundsel sellers, and turf cutters who sold turf mainly for food and roosting places for caged skylarks. Yet apart from costermongers none of these occupations features on the census records. Hollingshead (1861) states that the inhabitants were mainly poor labourers or the poorest costermongers. "Women if not laundresses are nothing at all and a mothers' society tries to teach them cooking and washing". Families of 5, 6, 10 or 12 were found leading a swinish life in one room even where they rented another. Dogs were bred for sale. The main vices were dirt, overcrowding and drunkenness. There were no known thieves or prostitutes because the lowest part was too poor!

While also painting a bleak picture, writing on the poor can be very unimaginative; it reported rather than conveyed experience. There were many pamphlets with statistical tables but "very rarely (if ever) do we confront anything resembling a self-actuating human being" (Pearson, 1983:178). Overcrowding is recounted, and the smell, but relationships and thoughts are not recorded. The writers were blind to complexities, comfortable in their moral certainty of what was to be done about the problem of the poor. Yet it was economic conditions, not 'moral or spiritual degradation', which determined the basic characteristics of life in poor communities.

It is much more rewarding to turn to the reminiscences, recorded by Morrell in the 1930s, of an old inhabitant of Agar Town born in 1851 and living in Cambridge Street until 1863. He stated that there were sports in Agar Fields, with its meadow and mulberry ground. Many people had their own houses with a little garden in front and one at the back. Street sellers would come round with hot mutton pies, penny pies and baked potatoes. The chief milkman, Mr Harvey, was ruined when Agar Town was destroyed. Weinreb and Hibbert (1983:8) record that Tom Sayers, the boxer, lived in Agar Town for many years.

Life was not unrelieved gloom for the Victorian poor. They helped each other, sharing goods, services and money, and relying on credit networks. Hollingshead (1861) had Agar Town inhabitants sharing what little they had. The inhabitants could also rely on the activities of zealous clergymen, particularly the Revd William Clemenger, whose soup kitchen was used as a cheap eating house. Hollingshead lists his successes in the 1850s – a temporary church, a mothers' society, a national school with 100 scholars, a Sunday school with 370 pupils, a penny bank, and a clothing fund – but dismisses these "attempts to supply physical deficiencies by showy educational and spiritual stop-gaps" (1861:161).

The census records

Census data will not re-create Agar Town but can at least give a fair idea of whether contemporary descriptions of the inhabitants were exaggerated. Poor Law records supplement this.

Looking at the 1851 census for Agar Town as a whole, at a period when the area was attracting attention as a notorious slum, one is struck by how 'ordinary' it appears. Those who were born in Ireland are very much the exception. There are no 'pig keepers' listed – common at the Potteries, North Kensington, a slum area with which Agar Town is often compared. Labourers and laundresses predominate in many streets but there are also 'respectable' trades, notably pianoforte makers, clerks, even an accountant and a jeweller. It is very unusual to find, at 12 Oxford Street, one Thomas Spalding, cats' meat dealer. In the further areas north of the Regent's Canal, such as Winchester Street, most of the houses were occupied by single families, at most by two; those in the main thoroughfare of Upper Cambridge Street had two or three. Lower Cambridge Street, the industrial centre of Agar Town, with many wharfs and a number of factories, had a few houses with dustmen and the only record of a scavenger. There were no Irish-born listed in this street.

Cambridge Crescent and Salisbury Crescent, described by contemporaries as the dirtiest part of a dirty district and which might therefore typify the shanty town image of Agar Town, repay careful attention. The *Household Words* article singles out these two streets, one said to be where the settlers were almost all shopkeepers, the poorest exhibiting a few apples and red herrings in their windows; the other "a few wretched hovels ranged in a slight curve" with huts of all shapes and sizes. The house of one family was said to be a large yellow van upon wheels, raised above "high mud mark".

Cambridge Crescent in 1851 had 69 households. There were costermongers, two brothers who dealt in tripe, vendors of horseflesh and fish sellers. Yet the majority were bricklayers or bricklayers' labourers. There were several carmen, a blacksmith, a wine cooper and a master japanner. Only one household head, Mary Maidment, born on the Isle of Wight, gave no occupation. Only three heads were born in Ireland (4%), and only one was born in St Giles. At the next census in 1861 Cambridge Crescent had sprouted a number of 'back cottages' and there were by then 79 households. Again, these were overwhelmingly in single-family occupation. There were four heads born in St Giles but no Irish-born. Only one person, in 'Back Cottage B' was described as a costermonger, but there were no fewer than 10 'general dealers'. There was one vendor of cats' meat and one hawker of fish. But there were many labourers and several bricklayers. 28 household heads were born outside London, but 64% had been born in the London area, with 26 (32%) born in St Pancras. It is interesting that William Duff, now aged 49, had moved from the three cottages which bore his name into a caravan (the *Household Words* yellow van?), and no longer a 'showman' was now a photographer.

In Salisbury Crescent in 1851 there were 39 households. There were no Irish-born at all and only one person born in St Giles. There were no costermongers or any 'unsavoury' occupations given. Apart from 7 general labourers, many were skilled men, eg historical engraver, stone mason, 2 plasterers, plumber, solicitor's clerk, 2 police constables, 4 fishing rod makers and 2 pianoforte makers. The picture is little different 10 years later. There were 38 households, and again no Irish-born. The range of occupations had grown. For example, there was an office beadle at University College, a whip maker, a cigar machinist, a coachsmith employing two boys and a policeman employed by the GNR.

The few Irish in Agar Town seem to have been concentrated in the heart of Agar Town, near the Oblique Bridge over the Canal. In 1851 at 13 Upper Cambridge Street the enumerator made a special note in the margin that there were six people in one room – this was clearly extremely unusual – a married bricklayer, his wife and daughter and three unmarried bricklayers, all born in Galway. There were in fact three other households at this address. Overcrowded, but a serious slum? Next door at No.14 lived just one family of three headed by a butcher.

In 1861, when Agar Town was at its greatest extent, there were 553 inhabited houses in Agar Town with 4057 people living there, split roughly equally north and south of the canal (2062 and 1995) and by sex (2071 males, 1986 females). The greengrocer's shop in Cambridge Street in 1857, Fig.13, looks in good repair and in neat surroundings.

Work

Almost every household head in Agar Town had an occupation listed on the census records. For male occupations labouring and building trades were the most common, but most women also worked – often taking in laundry. They were not "nothing at all". Children were normally shown as 'scholars', although the London City Mission Magazine (November 1846) felt that at an early age children in Agar Town were forced to make a living from street selling, or crime: according to this source, many were in prison and many were known to the police.

Costermongers formed a very small minority of people in Agar Town. Those who lived in Cambridge Crescent probably frequented the nearby Brill market in Somers Town, where "there is perhaps more business done than at any other spot of the same size in or near London" (*Old St Pancras Times*, 19 Jun 1858). Brill Market was forcibly closed in 1859, but Chapel Street market in Islington provided a substitute. Hollingshead wrote that there on Sundays the "stall keepers who crowd in the gutters with fish stalls and hardware stalls are mostly residents of Agar Town; and when they have done their business for the day they go home to their huts like merchants to their villas" (1861:142).

Pianoforte makers are quite noticeable on the census. The manufacture of pianos was centred on Camden Town to the north, taking advantage of the canal for bulk transportation of timber. There was also a fair sprinkling of railway workers because of the proximity of the GNR goods yard and King's Cross Station.

Poor Relief

The census records show barely anyone in receipt of parish relief, but then work was often seasonal. Poor Law records need to be checked to test Hollingshead's statement (1861) that Agar Town was a stepping stone to the workhouse. He said it was used as a sleeping place under the Act to entitle people to poor relief in St Pancras. The admissions registers for St Pancras Workhouse for the 12 months from June 1856 to May 1857 show that of the 3185 persons admitted 64, or a mere 2% of the total, gave addresses in Agar Town.

The position was scarcely different with outdoor relief. Parishes such as St Pancras that continued to give outdoor relief were likely to attract those displaced by railways and urban improvement. The treatment of those who received outdoor relief was extreme. Lees (1988:3) stresses that the benign picture of the downtrodden vanished in early Victorian times as views of poverty changed, Irish flooded into London and the separation of classes intensified. The poor were seen as outcast deviants, a threat to orderly life. Pauperism increased substantially during the 'hungry forties', becoming a major financial burden on rate payers. In St Pancras, the poor seeking outdoor relief had to wait outside the Vestry House from the early hours of the morning without shelter. Up to 900 people might gather. It could be 8 pm before relief was given, in the 'Black Hole', a room below the Vestry with foul air and disgusting conditions. The Vestry shared the utilitarian belief in poverty as immoral.

The GLRO has records of the examining committee for outdoor relief, whose main interest seems to have been to remove any person who claimed. I have checked through the records for 1862 to 1864. Only 8 families in Agar Town are recorded in this period, with none in 1864. For example, Emma Chambers aged 46 and her son aged 12 of 1 Durham Street West, considered to be irremovable by the settlement agent, were removed by the Committee. Most of the claimants were apparently deserted wives who were either ordered to be removed or failing that were admitted to the workhouse, a warrant being issued against their husband. I have also looked at the 'rough examinations' of the examining committee, which are manuscript biographical sketches of those applying for outdoor relief. These sketches reveal the great mobility of the working class at this time. In 1854 – the year I have studied in detail – there were roughly 350 entries for St Pancras, yet a mere 7 were from inhabitants of Agar Town.

More extensive study of the poor law records throughout the period of Agar Town's existence might reveal a different picture, but I am convinced that Agar Town was not such a desperate sink of poverty that significant numbers of its inhabitants either sought outdoor relief or admission to the Workhouse.

Health

The reports of the Board of Health into the cholera epidemics of 1849 and 1854 highlight certain slum areas such as The Potteries in North Kensington (where there was much pig-keeping and boiling of offal). While it records some deaths in Agar Town it passes over the area without comment.

Mr Hillier, The Medical Officer of Health for St Pancras, produced annual reports for the parish from 1856 until his death in 1867. The reports single out areas of high mortality or with poor or non-existent sewerage. Agar Town is not mentioned in this context at all. In 1856 Hillier was concerned about the "fearful state" of the roads "and there is no doubt that the constant moisture arising from them together with decomposing organic matter, exercises a very pernicious effect on the inhabitants" (p.14). In 1858 he notes the roads are in the same state but the Vestry has borrowed money for paving and he does not mention paving subsequently. In 1863 there was a smallpox outbreak in Agar Town in the streets adjoining the separation wards of St Pancras Workhouse, which he believed had been carried by the atmosphere for a considerable distance, in some cases up to 200 feet. Hillier records that in May 1863 there were 19 cases in Cambridge Street, Cambridge Row and Cambridge Crescent adding notably "before that date not a single case of smallpox had been heard of in these streets".

Conclusion

Agar Town was not the hellhole of contemporary description. A poor district, no doubt, but most of its inhabitants appear to have been in employment and relatively few had regular recourse to poor relief. Very few of its inhabitants had been born in Ireland, and very few seem to have relocated to Agar Town when the worst parts of St Giles were demolished. If it had been quite as awful as painted this should show up in health records, but it does not. That Agar Town was described as a sink of poverty and degradation suited the Midland Railway Company, since it justified their wholesale demolition of the district.

8: The railway and Agar Town

THE very earliest railway terminals had been sited some distance from the centre of London, using the cheapest and simplest approach and with minimum disturbance to property. After 1850 the railway companies sought to push their terminals further in, and they needed many acres for approach lines, sidings, marshalling yards, warehouses, engine sheds, forges, stabling and so on. The metropolitan extensions of the Midland Railway Company (MRC) in 1866 demolished 4000 houses in Somers, Camden and Agar Towns, displacing perhaps as many as 32,000 people (Dyos, 1982:102).

Railway companies often argued that demolition of slum property was a social improvement, and that railway lines let in light and air for the poor and gave better drainage. They obviously preferred to buy up slum property, since the poor had no legal standing. Compensation was provided by way of a lump sum or payment of rent arrears, but there was no legal obligation to give anything to weekly tenants, the majority of working-class inhabitants.

The plans of the MRC

During the 1850s the MRC decided that facilities at King's Cross were inadequate. It shared King's Cross and the line into it from Hitchin with the GNR. The MRC wanted its own goods station, where it could bring coal from Derbyshire and Nottinghamshire. The most promising location was a triangle of land at the northern end of Agar Town, bounded by the North London Railway, the GNR and the Regent's Canal, and including Elm Lodge and what was left of its grounds.

In February 1859 the MRC set up an Agar Town Committee, which in 6 months negotiated the purchase from the Ecclesiastical Commissioners of some 27 acres at the cost of £8,000. The price seems surprisingly low given that this was the 'better part of the town'. The formal indenture for the sale was not drawn up until June 1863 (Middx Reg 1863/16/892), but the Ecclesiastical Commissioners had clearly washed their hands of the area when in a letter of November 1860 they told the Vestry that it should now deal with the MRC.

Before work could begin on building the goods station, arrangements had to be made to find a new site for the church of Agar Town. The first church in Agar Town had been an iron chapel opened in 1847 during the rebuilding of St Pancras Old Church. A temporary church opened on 16 June 1850, a "neat little structure in the dirtiest part of the district" (HC BI 41) – on the corner of Cambridge Street and Cambridge Crescent. Other than the proceeds of the annual collection, this was maintained solely by the Agar family, who gave £65 p.a. (HC BI 39). In 1857 a school-church was built in Kingston Street; it opened on 19 November. Two years later, on 12 July 1859, the foundation stone of a permanent church, adjoining the school-church and designed by the architect S S Teulon, was laid by the Bishop of London.

But the church was never completed because the site was acquired by the MRC. A new parish church of St Thomas was to be erected at the MRC's expense, and the Midland Railway (London Station) Act 1860 provided for a site on a narrow strip of land between King's Road and the Regent's Canal. This provision was repealed by the Midland Railway (Additional Powers) Act 1861, which deemed that another site would be more convenient. The church of St Thomas, again designed by Teulon, was to be built by the Vicar partly out of the funds (£6,000) supplied by the Company for the erection of a church, school and parsonage. The existing schoolrooms and approaches in Kingston Street were not to be interfered with for 3 years unless other school rooms were erected meanwhile. They were. The new St Thomas' Church in Wrotham Road, Camden Town, was consecrated on 18 June 1863. This "immensely coarse" building (Pevsner, 1952) was demolished a century later.

The 1861 census reveals that the MRC were already building stores in Bolton Street. These are not separately identified on the Cassell map of 1862 (Fig.12), which is linked closely to the 1861 census, being a reprint of the Weller map of 1861. But the stores were rated at £300 on 3 December 1861. The Company's goods yard was gradually extended (1862-65) to cover most of the area north of the canal. The encroachment of the railway can already be clearly seen on the Stanford map of 1863 (Fig.14), which shows the MRC's goods yard and the coal yard encircling Elm Lodge. The sidings were extended across the canal, and a new bridge was built to carry the line into the Bass Ales Stores, begun after the demolition of Oxford Crescent and Durham Street in 1864.

The rest of Agar Town was also purchased in 1860 – although again the indentures were delayed (Middx Reg 1862/1/266 & 267) – on rather more demanding terms. All land to the east of Cambridge Street, including the cottages of Cambridge Crescent, 6 acres 3 roods in all, cost the MRC some £32,000. Wharf ground and premises along the Regent's Canal completed the purchase of the Agar Town estate at just under £50,000. William Barlow for the MRC then prepared parliamentary plans for the demolition of Agar Town.

The Vestry mounted an unsuccessful campaign against the MRC's plans. They had already petitioned the Commons on the Midland Railway (London Station) Bill in February 1860, mainly because of the potential loss in rates from the properties to be demolished, and the time it would take until the rateable value of the railway could be ascertained. They also wanted compensation for their expenditure on paving roads in the area. The Bill became law, but a special rating clause was included to make good local rates and in January 1861 the MRC agreed to pay to the Ecclesiastical Commissioners a quarter of the sum the Vestry had borrowed from them for road improvement.

In 1863 the MRC were authorised to extend their line from Bedford into London, but additional powers were needed to push this through Agar Town. The Midland Railway (St Pancras Branch) Bill, introduced in early 1864, was again opposed by the Vestry. Its main objection was the likely disruption to St Pancras Old Church graveyard. For the living the Vestry showed no such concern. On 11 January 1866 its members rejected a report from the Medical Officer urging them to take out a Public Works Loan and construct buildings for the poor.

The MRC's Bill became law and gave the MRC power to purchase lands and houses "by compulsion or agreement", authority to stop up or divert any roads, canals etc, and to raise share capital. £450,000 was to be raised in this way, and £150,000 through loans. The plans deposited show the line going under the North London Railway past the Midland sidings adjacent to it, in a swathe through Kingston and Durham Streets and Salisbury Crescent and over the Canal, obliterating Canterbury Terrace and Cambridge Crescent, across a corner of St Pancras burial ground, and over what was left of Canterbury Place. In the process all

Fig.14   Stanford map of 1863 (courtesy of Guildhall Library). Arrow, Elm Lodge

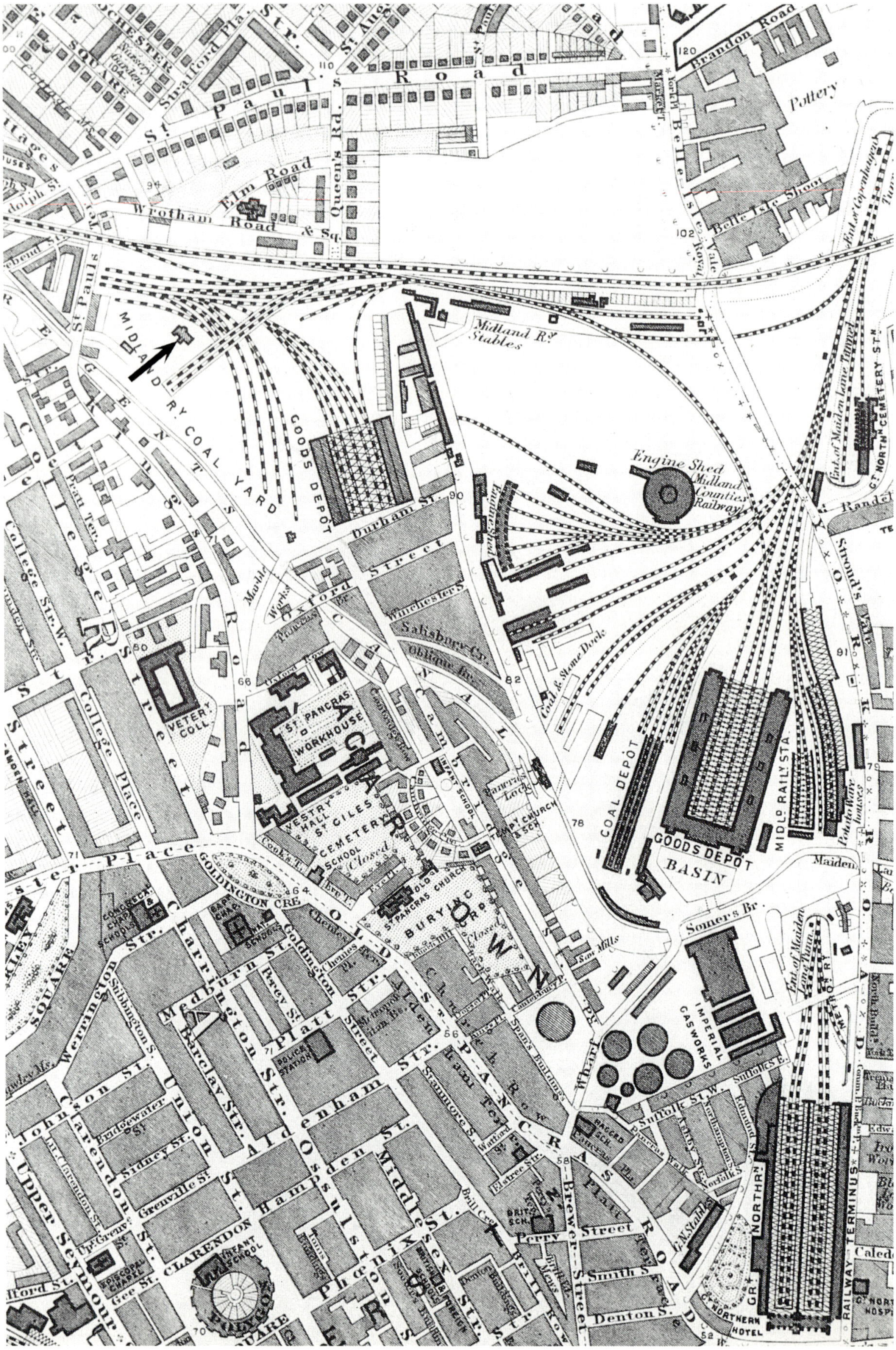

of Agar Town could be demolished.

By 1864 nearly all of the leases granted by the Agar family had expired, but the MRC would have had to compensate those who had taken out 99-year leases with the Ecclesiastical Commissioners. Also as owners the MRC would have had to pay for upkeep of the property even though they intended to demolish it. However, Mr Hillier, Medical Officer for Health, recorded that the MRC "still holds a considerable number [of houses] which it proposes to demolish, but in the meantime they are occupied and allowed to fall into a very dilapidated and unwholesome state" (Annual Report 1862:6).

Although weekly tenants could be evicted without compensation the overall cost of demolition of Agar Town and much of Somers Town and the construction of the St Pancras line was huge. In 1867 MRC shareholders were told that an extra £2,150,000 was needed. The value of the property and amount of compensation had been much more than anticipated (Coppock & Prince, 1964:128).

The contract (value £319,000) for the St Pancras extension was awarded to Waring Brothers on 12 February 1866. Within days the demolition of Agar Town began. By April Agar Town was no more.

The dispersal of the inhabitants

There was no public regret at the destruction of Agar Town. "Our thanks... for having cleared away the whole, or nearly the whole of the above mentioned district of mud and hovels" (Walford, 1987, V:370).

There was no mention in the local paper, *The Camden and Kentish Towns Gazette*. The paper did report regularly during 1866 on the numbers of indoor poor at the workhouse, which were consistently about 200 up on 1865, but a committee report (July 7) put the increase down to the inadequate amount paid in outdoor relief. Mr Hillier, the Medical Officer of Health, in his last annual report in 1867 noted that "very serious inconveniences have been suffered by the poor who were ejected" (3).

Where did the displaced go? Opinions vary. Miller records in 1874 that casuals or the homeless poor were squatting outside the Workhouse, many of the remaining four-roomed houses in Somers Town were crowded with those who used to live in streets now occupied by the MRC station, and that "hundreds are crowding and lowering the character of Kentish Town, and others have taken up quarters in Islington" (Miller, 1874:59). Richardson notes that Camden Town had a "great influx of the lower classes" after the demolition of Agar Town (1991:119). Tindall (1980:173) states that the people crowded into the northern part of the parish, notably in Kentish Town, where the Gazette talked of riff-raff and illegitimate babies.

One benefit of the demolition of Agar Town, alongside many other railway schemes in the 1860s, was that it highlighted the problem of working-class housing in central London and strengthened calls for cheap fares to make suburban living possible for the working class. As an 1866 editorial in *The Working Man* asked, "Why don't they build us a great village or town out Epping way... and then let the railways bring us backwards and forwards for a trifle? They take our homes; let them give us something in return" (in Dyos, 1982:113).

9: Agar town: an assessment

THE end for Agar Town was swift and merciless, a vivid example of the havoc railways wreaked in working-class areas. The MRC argued that they were performing a service to the metropolis.

It is always easy in hindsight to say that conditions were not so bad as they were made out. Agar Town had inadequate drainage, was neither paved nor lit, had at best an intermittent water supply, and was in not very salubrious surroundings. Some of the buildings run up in the 1840s were built very cheaply and may not have been sound. Some of its population was very poor.

But it was not the illegal shanty town of popular imagination. Working men took out leases from the Agar family. They did so against a background of chronic housing shortage. Here was an opportunity to build one's home in a new 'suburban' area within walking distance of employment and markets. If the covenants in the lease – which specified room size and construction – were followed the houses would have been of above-average size for working-class property. The builders probably skimped because this was common practice, although the rateable values of Agar Town properties were often greater than working-class property elsewhere in London. This reflected the range of property on the Estate and in this, as in so many other respects, surviving records show that Agar Town was unremarkable.

The make-up of its population was also very similar to other working-class areas. I can find no evidence to back up the dire picture provided by the social topographers. Most of its inhabitants appear to have been in employment, and recourse to parish poor relief appears to have been low. If this was really the "suburban Connemara" of the *Household Words* article, Irish would have predominated in the census records, whereas Irish-born people are notable by their relative absence.

Victorian social topographers had an angle. They were describing conditions in areas unknown to their readers so as to effect change. Hollingshead's *Ragged London*, for example, was "an attempt to beat the bounds of metropolitan dirt and misery" (1861:v), which he considered a national disgrace. He and other writers were using images of social degradation to define issues and press goals: what Mayne has called "slumland sensationalism as a catalyst for legislative reform" (1993:140).

By the 1850s, with the failure of Chartism and the end of the cholera epidemic, the initial shock value of slums had worn off and general interest waned. Sanitary reformers gained only a small and relatively specialised readership. There was only sporadic interest in the daily press, unlike the later mass interest in the 1880s and 1890s. The influence of reformers was greatest when it overlapped with entertaining sensationalism of journalists writing about low life. Indeed, *Ragged London* developed from a series of articles for *The Morning Post*. Mayhew popularised the concept that slums were as little known as the wilds of Africa – geographical proximity, yet moral distance. The language of travel and exploration was always used, and life in slums was presented as lethargic and directionless. Activity was illicit, drunken and nocturnal. The elimination of hovels meant progress, the stamping out not just of infectious disease but of moral disease – violence, robbery and vice. "The storyline for slumland necessarily ends in judgment" (Mayne, 1993:184), its destruction a blessing. And so it was when Agar Town was demolished in 1866.

Damer argues that the Victorian capitalist state was not interested in the very poor, or *lumpenproletariat*, since there were sufficient numbers of the working class to form its 'industrial reserve army'. He writes that the State deliberately fostered the fragmentation of the working class and demoralised or criminalised the very poor, who were stigmatised as undeserving. "The cornerstone of bourgeois ideology about slum dwellers was to represent them as in some sense responsible for their situation" (1989:80). He notes that the poor were caricatured, and a sensational literature "concentrated on murder, prostitution and debauchery at the expense of the material determinants of their life" (1989:39).

Whether or not one accepts Damer's Marxist interpretation of the role of the State, it is undeniable that contemporary accounts of Agar Town were sensationalist, and surviving records simply do not support the more dramatic descriptions of the housing reformers and social topographers. Agar Town was unfairly 'labelled'. If this is true of Agar Town, notorious as a slum area at the time, how true might it be of other infamous districts of Victorian London?

An undated manuscript note in the Heal Collection records that Lord Grosvenor, for one, did not find Agar Town so bad as described. He had just walked through Agar Town with the Vicar and the Revd William Clemenger. He saw some neat back gardens. "The people were poor but hard working" (HC BI 38). The surviving records bear out this assessment rather than lurid accounts of a foul slum housing a depraved population. Agar Town does not deserve its reputation.

10: Agar town today

Fig.15 Camley Street Natural Park (1995)

AFTER the MRC had constructed its goods yard and then its line into the new St Pancras station there was virtually nothing remaining of Agar Town. Elm Lodge was demolished by the MRC in 1867. A few buildings were left nearby, along the east side of King's Road (now St Pancras Way), one of which still stands. This is the public house, *The Constitution*, built by Thomas Bolton on a plot on which he had taken a 99-year lease from 5 March 1853 at £10 per annum (Middx Reg 1854/6/9).

The one remaining road in Agar Town was Cambridge Street, although its course was diverted under the new railway line before it swung round to meet the Oblique Bridge, now replaced by a concrete and steel 'replica' of the original cast-iron structure. Along Cambridge Street were the coalshoots of both the MRC (on its western side) and the GNR. The latter was the brainchild of Samuel Plimsoll (1824-98) of 'Plimsoll Line' shipping fame. He had patented a coal drop which was successfully tried out within the GNR goods yard on the opposite bank of the canal. The goods yard's boundaries were extended in 1865 when houses, stables and canalside wharves fronting Cambridge Street were cleared and a viaduct on iron girders was built across the canal by Plimsoll. Gilbert (1985) has described the operation of the coal depot in Camley Street (as Cambridge Street was later renamed). Below the railway line was a series of bays, each rented by a different coal merchant. Wagons were pulled over the correct bay by a capstan and coal was tipped down a chute for bagging up below, then (still in the bay) loaded onto a cart and taken off for distribution.

Just to the north of the coalshoots the St Pancras Basin was excavated in 1867 and opened as a coal wharf for the MRC. It was used for unloading ash from their locomotives into barges which were taken up the canal to tips at Cowley. In July 1961 the St Pancras Yacht Club was founded and the basin was fitted out for use. It is now the St Pancras Yacht Basin, private HQ of the club.

As the 20th century progressed the railway ceased to need its vast goods yards, especially with the post-war decline in the demand for coal. In Camley Street the two coalshoots were shut down, and demolished in the 1960s. The former MRC coalshoot became a municipal rubbish tip. That of the GNR was also used as a tip, although unofficially, and became largely colonised by wild flowers. The GLC eventually stepped in. After discarding plans for a coach park on the site it began the creation of Camley Street Natural Park (Fig.15) in 1983. The Park opened in 1984. During site clearance many fragments of Victorian pottery and oystershells were found, evidence of earlier occupation when this was part of Agar Town.

The problem of the many acres of 'railway lands' in the hinterland of King's Cross still bedevils planners today. Part of these lands – what had been the MRC's goods yard built over Agar Town – came into the possession of the London Borough of Camden. From the mid-1970s a number of uses for the site were considered. In September 1975 Camden Council gave approval for 6 acres to form the new Elm Village which would house nearly 3000 residents of the borough. These early plans came to naught and there were complaints in the press of vandalism and fly-tipping in the area. In 1978 Rupert Murdoch's *News International* was considering 8 acres of the site for a £30m headquarters building, but in the end moved to Wapping. In early 1980 the Council thought about using the land for a temporary gypsy caravan site. In the same year the Department of Environment refused a loan sanction for council housing.

Much of the site was subsequently sold for mixed development of housing association and private housing: the present-day Elm Village. The housing developed by Fairview Estates was opened in March 1984 when Councillor Ron Hefferman planted a flowering ash. The name Elm Village of course recalls Elm Lodge, whose grounds once covered the site. The architects of the estate – which won a Golden Jubilee Award from the Housing Centre Trust in 1984 for outstanding housing achievement – may well have known something of the area's history. Looking down Bergholt Mews today towards the white, slightly classical-looking buildings at the end, one can recreate in one's mind the approach to Elm Lodge, which stood just here: before the canal, before the railway and before Agar Town.

Annex 1 Article in *Household Words*, 8 March 1851, by W.M.Thomas

A suburban Connemara

I was born and bred in Manchester. My earliest impression—which has hardly left me yet—that all rich men are mill-owners, and all poor men and women merely spinners. I am proud of being a Manchester man, for there is not a town more orderly or better lighted and paved, or (till lately) better swept, in England. Till I was four-and-twenty I had never been out of my native town. Early and late I toiled in my father's counting-house, without ever thinking of stirring out of it, or taking a holiday; for my father used to say, that God gave man one day out of every seven for rest, and He knew what was enough for him. I used to hear of London at that time, and to fancy that Watling Street was a kind of High Street to the Metropolis; for all our correspondents dated from Watling Street. When the railway opened, there came a great change in this respect. I made my first journey to London and finding that I knocked off a good deal of business by the transaction, I began to run up to town nearly every week, which I have continued to do ever since.

Thus, though I am a Manchester man, I know the City as well as any Londoner. I know every court and alley of it, and can make short cuts, and find the nearest way from any one part of that great labyrinth to another. I confess I am not so well acquainted with the suburbs. I had always a favourable impression of the northern side of London, from the pretty villas and cottages which I had remarked on each side of the line, on coming up by the North-Western Railway. Therefore, having lately found it advisable to transfer my business altogether to Watling Street, City, I resolved to seek in that quarter for a residence for myself and family.

Another reason induced me to select that spot. My goods are coming up continually by the North Western Railway; and having some commissions in the West Riding, who send up parcels by the Great Northern line, I wished to be somewhere between Battle Bridge and Euston Square: in order, occasionally, to give an eye to my consignments at both stations. With this purpose I procured a new map, on a large scale, in order to see all the Victoria Crescents and Albert Terraces thereabouts.

I drew out my pocket-compasses, measured the line, reduced it one half; and, on finding the unknown locality, brought one point of the dividor's plumb upon a spot which I at once read off from the map as "Agar Town." Looking more minutely, I observed that the particular point of the district indicated, was "Salisbury Crescent." I could not repress an exclamation of satisfaction as Oxford and Cambridge Crescents also met my eye. Without further delay, I struck a half-mile circle; and as I observed therein several streets and terraces bearing the names, Canterbury, Winchester, Durham, Salisbury, &c., I concluded that this was (as it eventually turned out to be) Church property; and, as a lover of order and decency, I congratulated myself on the felicitous idea that had suggested to me that neighbourhood; for I felt this circumstance to be a guarantee of an orderly and well-regulated estate.

From these high-sounding names, however, I had some misgivings that the houses in that neighbourhood might be of too expensive a class for a man of moderate means. Still, I resolved to proceed there and reconnoitre, in the hope of finding a decent little place, at a moderate figure. So, with my map in my hand, I rode down to King's Cross, and proceeding along the old Pancras Road, entered the King's Road, which is the boundary of the property I was seeking. I had not gone far beyond a large building, which I found was the St. Pancras Workhouse, when I observed a woman and a number of ragged children drawing a truck. The truck contained a table, two or three old chairs, and some kitchen utensils, with a large bundle of bed-clothes tied up in a patchwork quilt. The entire strength of the company was exerted to draw the truck up the steep pathway of a turning on the right-hand side of the road, in which they succeeded at length; and the woman, struggling, with her hair about her face, and her bonnet hanging round her neck, the truck moved on, aided by the vigorous pushing of her young family behind. The pathway is some feet above the road, which was a complete bog of mud and filth, with deep cart-ruts; the truck, oscillating and bounding over the inequalities of the narrow pathway, threatened every moment to overturn with the woman, her family, and all her worldly goods.

There was something so painfully picturesque in the little group, and so exciting in the constant apprehension of an accident, that I could not help following. For a time, however, a special Providence seemed to watch over the party. I began to give up all fear of a mishap – when, suddenly, the inner wheel encountered a small hillock of dust and vegetable refuse at the door of a cottage, and finally shot its contents into the deep slough of the roadway. The woman turned back; and, having well thumped the heads of her family, seated herself upon the heap of ashes which had been the cause of her misfortune, to vent the rest of her rage in abuse of a miscellaneous character.

A dustman happening to pass at the time, helped the children to restore the chattels to the righted truck.

"How fur have you to go?" he asked.

"Oh! not fur," said she, "only to one of them cottages yonder. It's very aggravatin', arter draggin' them goods all the way from Smithses Rents, and all along that there nasty road, all right; just to upset when one's got here ! This ain't no woman's work, this ain't; only my husband's got a job this mornin', and we was obliged to move out afore twelve which is the law, they says."

"What is the name of this place?" I asked.

"This here, sir ?" replied the woman; "why, Hagar Town."

"Agar Town?" I exclaimed, with astonishment, remembering how clean and promising it had appeared upon the map. "Do you mean to say that I am really in Agar Town?"

The dustman, who by this time had finished his job, and who sat upon the pathway smoking a short black pipe with his legs dangling over the road, like a patient angler by a very turbid stream, ventured to join the conversation, by answering my question.

"You're as nigh," said he, "to the middle o' Hager Town as you vell can be."

"And where" said I, "is Salisbury Crescent?"

"There's Salisbury Crescent!"

I looked up, and saw several wretched hovels, ranged in a slight curve, that formed some excuse for the name. The doors were blocked up with mud, heaps of ashes, oyster-shells, and decayed vegetables.

"It's a rum place, ain't it?" remarked the dustman. "I am forced to come through it twice every day, for my work lays that way; but I wouldn't, if I could help it. It don't much matter in my business, a little dirt, but Hagar Town is worse nor I can abear."

"Are there no sewers?"

"Sooers? Why, the stench of a rainy morning is enough fur to knock down a bullock. It's all very well for them as is lucky enough to have a ditch afore their doors; but, in gen'ral, everybody chucks everythink out in front and there it stays. There used to be inspector of noosances, when the choleray was about; but, as soon as the choleray went away, people said they didn't want no more of that suit till such times as the choleray should break out agen."

"Is the whole of Agar Town in such a deplorable state as this?" I asked.

"All on it! Some places, wuss. You can't think what rookeries there is in some parts. As to the roads, they ain't never been done nothink to. *They* ain't roads. I recollect when this place was all gardeners' ground; it was a nice pooty place enough then. That ain't above ten or twelve year ago. When people began to build on it, they run up a couple o' rows o' houses oppersite one another, and then the road was left fur to make itself. Then the rain come down, and people chucked their rubbidge out; and the ground beln' nat' rally soft, the carts from the brick-fields worked it all up into paste."

"How far does Agar Town extend?" I asked.

"Do you see them cinder heaps out a yonder?"

I looked down in the distance, and beheld a lofty chain of dark mountains.

"Well," said the Dustman, "that's where Hagar Town ends – close upon Battle Bridge. Them heaps is made o' breeze; breeze is the siftins of the dust what has been put there by the conteractor's men, arter takin' away all the wallyables as has been found."

At this point, the woman, who had been combing her hair, arose, and the truck resumed its perilous journey. The dustman waited, and saw it arrive at its destination, in safety; whereupon the dustman having smoked his pipe, departed. As I had, by this time, given up all intention of seeking a residence in that neighbourhood, I continued my researches like Dr. Syntax, simply in search of the picturesque.

Crossing another bridge—for the canal takes a winding course through the midst of this Eden—I stood beside the Good Samaritan public-house, to observe the houses which the dustman had pointed out, with the water "a flowin' in at the back doors." Along the canal side, the huts of the settlers, of many shapes and sizes, were closely ranged. Every tenant, having, as I was informed, his own lease of the ground, appeared to have disdained to imitate his neighbour, and to have constructed his abode according to his own ideas of beauty or convenience. There were the dog-kennel, the cow-shed, the shanty, and the elongated watch-box, styles, of architecture. To another, the ingenious residence of Robinson Crusoe seemed to have given his idea. Through an opening was to be seen another layer of dwellings, at the back: one looking like a dismantled windmill, and another, perched upon a wall, like a guard's look-out on the top of a railway carriage. The love of variety was, everywhere, carried to the utmost pitch of extravagance. Every garden had its nuisance – so far the inhabitants were agreed – but, every nuisance was of a distinct and peculiar character. In the one, was a dung-heap; in the next, a cinder-heap; in a third, which belonged to the cottage of a costermonger, were a pile of whelk and periwinkle shells, some rotten cabbages, and a donkey; and the garden of another, exhibiting a board inscribed with the words "Ladies' School," had become a pond of thick green water, which was carefully dammed up, and prevented from flowing over upon the canal towing-path, by a brick parapet.

I remember to have seen, in a book written some time since, a chapter devoted to the *beau idéal* of an English villa and estate. The village church was, at that period, considered of some importance, and an approach thereto by a good road was treated as an element in securing the comfort and well-being of the villagers I looked for the "heaven-directing spire," and thought of the bogs, sloughs, and quagmires that must, necessarily, be struggled through by a pious parishioner; and I wondered whether it was possible for any amount of courage and patience to prevail over the difficulties. The English Captain, who attended church at San Francisco, in fisherman's mud-jacks, with trowsers close reefed up each leg, felt all his misgivings at his grotesque appearance vanish when he saw other men dressed like himself, and observed that the prevailing costume for ladies was Wellington boots; but, I should like to know what sympathy an inhabitant of Agar Town would get, if, on a Sunday morning, he presented himself before the parish beadle thus attired! The Rector of St. Pancras has endeavoured to meet his parishioners in this district, half-way; for, finding the difficulty of moving Agar Town to church, he moved the church to Agar Town; and a neat little structure, or temporary church, is now conveniently planted in the dirtiest part of the district.

The inhabitants themselves exhibit a genuine Irish apathy. Here and there, a barrow or two of oyster shells, broken bricks, and other dry materials, have been thrown into the mud. In Cambridge Row, I observed that some effort had been made to get a crossing; but, a sign-board indicated that it was to facilitate the approach to "The back door of the Good Samaritan."

Continuing my way until I came within the shadow of the great cinder-heaps of Mr. Darke, the contractor, I turned off at Cambridge Crescent, to make the hazardous attempt of discovering a passage back into the Pancras Road. At the corner of Cambridge Crescent are the Talbot Arms Tea Gardens, boasting a dry skittle-ground, which, if it be not an empty boast, must be an Agar Town island. The settlers of Cambridge Crescent are almost all shopkeepers –the poorest exhibiting in their rag-patched windows a few apples and red-herrings, with the rhyming announcement, "Table-beer, Sold here." I suspect a system of barter prevails – the articles sold there comprehending, no doubt, the whole of the simple wants of the inhabitants; a system, perhaps, suggested by the difficulty of communication with the civilised world.

A stranger in these parts immediately attracts the attention of the neighbourhood; and if he be not recognised for an Agarite, is at once set down for a "special commissioner," about to report to some newspaper upon the condition of the inhabitants. I met no one having the air of a stranger, except an unlucky gentleman, attempting to make a short cut to the London and York Railway station and a postman, vainly inquiring for Aurora Cottage. There were Bath, and Gloucester, Roscommon, Tralee, and Shamrock Cottages; but Aurora Cottage, being probably in some adjoining street, was entirely unknown to the mud-bound inhabitants. The economy of space which I had observed from the bridge, was also apparent here. Every corner of a garden contained its hut, well stocked with dirty children. The house of one family was a large yellow van upon wheels, thus raised above high mud-mark. This was the neatest dwelling I had observed. It had two red painted street-doors, with bright brass knockers, out of a tall man's reach, and evidently never intended for knocking – the entrance being by steps at the head of the van; indeed, I suspect that these doors were what the stage managers call "impracticable." The interior appeared to be well furnished, and divided into bed-room and sitting-room. Altogether, it had a comfortable look, with its chimney-pipe smoking on the top; and if I were doomed to live in Agar Town, I should certainly like lodgings in the yellow van.

As I proceeded, my way became more perilous. The footpath, gradually narrowing, merged at length in the bog of the road. I hesitated; but, to turn back was almost as dangerous as to go on. I thought, too, of the possibility of my wandering through the labyrinth of rows and crescents until I should be benighted; and the idea of a night in Agar Town, without a single lamp to guide my footsteps, emboldened me to proceed. Plunging at once into the mud, and hopping in the manner of a kangaroo – so as not to allow myself time to sink and disappear altogether – I found myself, at length, once more in the King's Road.

It is not my wish to inquire into the affairs of the ground landlords, or to attempt to guess at their reasons for allowing such a miserable state of things to exist upon their property. I have understood that the fee of the estate is in the Ecclesiastical Commissioners, and that the present owners hold it only for a term of three lives; with a power of leasing for periods not longer than twenty-one years each. If this be the case, perhaps no respectable tenant could be induced to take the land for so short a term upon a building lease. Yet, when it is considered how much it would have been for the benefit of all parties that decent and comfortable dwellings should have occupied the ground instead of the wretched huts to be found there, it is much to be regretted that some arrangement was not entered into for that purpose. The place, in its present state, is a disgrace to the metropolis. It has sprung up in about ten years. Old haunts of dirt and misery, suffered to exist in times when the public paid no attention to such matters, are difficult to deal with; but this is a new evil, which only began to come into existence about the time when Mr. Chadwick's Report first brought before the public a picture of the filthy homes and habits of the labouring classes, and of the frightful amount of crime and misery resulting therefrom.

In Agar Town we have within a short walk of the City—not a gas-light panorama of Irish misery, "almost as good as being there," but a perfect reproduction of one of the worst towns in Ireland. The land is well situated – being high for the most part – and therefore capable of good drainage, and, although too great a proximity to the cinder-heaps might make it an objectionable site for a superior class of dwellings, no spot could be better adapted for the erection of small tenements for labouring men and mechanics. It is close to the terminus of one of the great trunk railways, where a large number of men – officers of the company and labourers – are employed. There are, also, many large manufactories in the neighbourhood. The men employed in these places must reside near their work, and are consequently compelled to take any accommodation, however miserable, which the neighbourhood may afford, and at whatever cost. A respectable mechanic told me that he paid for his hut a rent of six shillings per week. This contained two rooms only – upon the ground, for there was no upper story. It appeared to have hardly any foundation, the boards of the floor being laid upon the earth, without a brick between, to prevent the dampness oozing through; a manner of building which has been repeatedly pointed out, by the Sanitary Commissioners, as productive of disease. The place was altogether of the rudest and most comfortless description, and could not, I was I assured, have cost more in the erection – built as it was of old fragments of brick and plaster – than forty pounds.

It was not by choice, but by necessity, that this man lived in such a place. In various parts, a certain air of cleanliness in a dwelling, here and there, contrasting with the filthy state of the street, gave evidence of other inhabitants who had not been led by a mere taste for filth and wretchedness to take up their abode in Agar Town. These poor people cannot help themselves; toiling early and late, the struggle to provide for the ever-renewing wants of the day, exacts all their time and energies. Who will help them?

Annex 2 Ground rents in York Place and Canterbury Place

Diagrammatic representation of the area of study in Chapter 6. Plot size to scale. The numbers in **bold** refer to the agreements in the GLRO deeds papers. Names are the lease-holders of the plots, with the year they took on the lease.

Ground rents for the plots
Letters refer to plots shown on the diagram. Plots A to P amounted to 0.88 acre, at a rate which gave the Agar family £76 2s 6d an acre.

Plot	Ground rent	Size in feet
A	£7 12s	76 × 56
B	£3	76 × 24
C	£4	77 × 32
D	£4	76 × 32
E	£8	72 × 64
F	£4	70 × 32
G	£4	72 × 32
H	£3	70 × 22
I	£2 10s	70 × 20
J	£2 10s	70 × 20
K	£4	70 × 32
L	£4 10s	72 × 36
M	£4	72 × 32
N	£3 18s	72 × 31
O	£4 10s	72 × 34
P	£4	72 × 30
(Q	£5 4s	..........)

Kings Place

Canterbury Place side:

1272
1 — Alpha Cottages
1840 Alexander Young
    Sarah Penfold
1856 Sarah Le Petit

2 — 1840 Alexander Young
        Sarah Penfold

3 — Alpha Cottages

4 —

A

1271
5 — 1840 Thomas Hall

B

1300/1306/1315 — Hope Cottages
6 — 1840 Thomas Vickers, Jr
    1843 Thomas Clarke & Robert Wilkie
    1852 Wm Blunt
7 — 1857 Walter Capon (moiety)

C

1294/1298/1302
8 — 1840 Thomas Vickers, Sr
    1842 Wm Ralph
    1847 Edward Wilson-Howson
9 — 1851 Wm Blunt

D

1290/1302/1304/1305
10 — 1842 Thomas Vickers, Sr
     1842 Wm Ralph
     1847 Edward Wilson-Howson
     1850 Thomas H Devonshire
11 — 1851 Wm Blunt

12 — 1842 Thomas Vickers, Sr

13 —

14 —

E

1280/1281/1296
15 — 1841 Henry Kelly
     1842 John Pater
     1842 James Smith
        Eliza Smith
16 —

F

1287/1309
17–22 (renamed 1–5 Parham Place)
1841 Stephen Capon

G

York Place side:

1273/1307
1840 Edward Manion
1862 Samuel Le Petit
H — 16

1275 — Hearne Cottages
1840 Thomas Dodds
1842 Samuel Le Petit
I — 15

1276 — Grape Vine Cottages
1840 James Hoyle
1858 Mary Ann Hoyle
J — 14

1279/1263
1840 Henry Pearn
1851 Wm Blunt
K — 13

— 12

1255/1260/1261 — 1–4 David Cottages
1840 Thomas Vickers, Sr
1841 Joshua Wardle
1844 Hannah Wardle
1851 Wm Blunt
— 11
— 10
— 9
1844 A Cameron
1852 H Blunt
L — 8A

1256/1297
1841 John Bannister
1843 Wm Blunt
1844 Hugh Blunt
— 8

1848 Wm Blunt
— 7
M

1286/1307
1841 Chas Hiscox
1854 Wm Blunt
— 6

— 5
N

1253/1289/1266
1841 James Johnson
    Thomas Johnson
1854 Hugh Blunt
1857 Wm Blunt
— 4
— 3

1851 Wm Hobson
1854 Hugh Blunt
1857 Wm Blunt
O — 2

1299
1841 James North
    GNR
— 1

P

Q — GNR

31

Bibliography

19th-Century Material

T. Beames, *The Rookeries of London* (1852)

G. Clinch, *Marylebone and St Pancras* (1890)

H. Gavin, *The Habitations of the Industrial Classes* (1850, repr. 1985)

H. Gavin, *The Unhealthiness of London* (1847, repr. 1985)

G. Godwin, *Town Swamps and Social Bridges* (1859, repr. 1972)

J. Hole, *The Homes of the Working Classes* (1866)

J. Hollingshead, *Ragged London in 1861* (1861)

F. Miller, *St Pancras Past and Present* (1874)

S. Palmer, *St Pancras* (1870)

M. Schlesinger, *Saunterings in London* (1853)

Major Gen G. B. Tremenheere, *Dwellings of the Labouring Classes of the Metropolis* (1856)

E. Walford, *Old and New London* (1872), reprinted as *London Recollected*, vol. V (1987)

F. S. Williams, *The Midland Railway : Its Rise and Progress* (1875)

S. Wiswould, *Charitable Foundations of St Pancras* (1863)

Parliamentary Material

PP, 1850, Board of Health, 2, *Report on the Cholera Epidemic*

PP, 1851, XXIII, *Report lately made to the Board of Health in reference to the sanitary condition of Agar Town by R. D. Grainger*

PP, 1854-55, XLV, *Board of Health Report on Epidemic Cholera in 1854*

PP, 1854-55, XLV, *Board of Health Report on the Common and Model Lodging Houses of the Metropolis by C. Glover*

PP, 1857-88, IX, *Reports from Committees, Evidence to the Lords Select Committee on the means of Divine Worship in Populous Districts*

Annual Reports of the Ecclesiastical Commissioners (1859-1867), especially PP 1861, XLVIII and PP, 1864, XVIII

Report of the Board of Trade into *Metropolitan Railways Schemes*, 9 Feb 1864

Secondary Sources

E. G. Barnes, *The Rise of the Midland Railway 1844-1874* (1966)

A. R. Bennett, *London and Londoners in the 1850s and 1860s* (1924)

G. Best, *Mid-Victorian London 1851-70* (1979)

W. E. Brown, *St Pancras Open Spaces and Disused Burial Grounds* (1902)

J. Burnett, *A Social History of Housing 1815-1970* (1986)

S. Chapman, *The History of Working Class Housing : A Symposium* (1971)

G. E. Cherry, *Cities and Plans* (1988)

L. Clarke, *Building Capitalism* (1992)

J. T. Coppock and H. C. Prince, *Greater London* (1964)

G. Crossick, *An Artisan Elite in Victorian Society: Kentish London 1840-1880* (1978)

S. Damer, *From Moorepark to 'Wine Alley': The rise and fall of a Glasgow housing scheme* (1989)

M. J. Daunton, *House and Home in the Victorian City* (1983)

C. Denyer, *St Pancras Through The Centuries* (1935)

H. J. Dyos, *Exploring The Urban Past* (1982)

H. J. Dyos, *Victorian Suburb: A Study of the Growth of Camberwell* (1977)

H. J. Dyos and M. Wolff (eds.), *The Victorian City: Images and Realities* (1973)

M. Essex-Lopresti, *Exploring The Regent's Canal* (1987)

S. M. Gaskell, *Slums* (1990)

E. Gauldie, *Cruel Habitations : A History of Working Class Housing 1790-1918* (1974)

R. Gilbert, *The King's Cross Cut : A City Canal and its Community* (1985)

R. Glass (ed.), *London: Aspects of Change* (1964)

D. George, *London Life in the Eighteenth Century* (1965)

D. Green, *People of the Rookery: A Pauper Community in Victorian London* (1986)

M. Hunter and R. Thomas (eds.), *Change at King's Cross* (1990)

R. Hyde, *Printed Maps of Victorian London 1851-1900* (1975)

G. S. Jones, *Outcast London* (1984)

J. R. Kellett, *Impact of the Railways on Victorian Cities* (1969)

C. E. Lee, *St Pancras Church and Parish* (1955)

L. Lees, *Poverty and Pauperism in Nineteenth Century London* (1988)

A. Mayne, *The Imagined Slum: Newspaper Representation in Three Cities 1870-1914* (1993)

Rev. R. C. Morrell, *The Story of Agar Town: The Ecclesiastical Parish of St Thomas, Camden Town* (1935)

D. J. Olsen, *The City as a Work of Art* (1986)

D. J. Olsen, *The Growth of Victorian London* (1976)

D. J. Olsen, *Town Planning in London : The Eighteenth and Nineteenth Centuries* (1964)

G. Pearson, *Hooligan: A History of Respectable Fears* (1983)

N. Pevsner, *Buildings of England. London 2: except the Cities of London and Westminster* (1952)

J. Richardson, *Camden Town and Primrose Hill* (1991)

F. Sheppard, *London 1808-1870: The Infernal Wen* (1971)

J. Simmons, *St Pancras Station* (1968)

F. Sinclair, *Catalogue of An Exhibition and Display Illustrating St Pancras Through the Ages* (1938)

H. Spencer, *London's Canal: The History of the Regent's Canal* (1961)

Survey of London, Vol XIX: Old St Pancras and Kentish Town (1938)

J. N. Tarn, *Working Class Housing in Nineteenth Century Britain* (1971)

F. M. L. Thompson (ed.), *The Rise of Suburbia* (1982)

G. Tindall, *The Fields Beneath* (1980)

B. Weinreb and C. Hibbert, *The London Encyclopaedia* (1983)

A. S. Wohl, *The Eternal Slum* (1977)

J. Yelling, *Slums and Slum Clearance in Victorian London* (1986)

Articles

R. Conquest, "The Black Hole of St Pancras", *Camden History Review* 3, 1975, pp. 19-24

P. E. Malcolmsen, "Getting a living in the slums of Victorian Kensington", *London Journal* 1, May 1975